CULINARY CONTENT MANAGER: Catherine Pelletier

AUTHORS: Benoit Boudreau and Richard Houde

CHEFS: Benoit Boudreau and Richard Houde

FOOD STYLIST SUPERVISOR: Christine Morin

PHOTOGRAPHERS: Mélanie Blais, Tony Davidson, Rémy Germain
and Marie-Ève Lévesque

PHOTOGRAPHER AND VIDEOGRAPHER: Francis Gauthier

COLLABORATORS: Sabrina Belzil, Louise Bouchard, Ève Godin, Martin Houde,
Jessie Marcoux, Patricia Tremblay and Perfection Design Communication

TRANSLATION: Edgar

LEGAL DEPOSIT: 2nd quarter 2018
Bibliothèque et Archives nationales du Québec
National Library and Archives of Canada
ISBN 978-2-89658-812-1

(Original edition: ISBN 978-2-89658-809-1, Éditions Pratico-pratiques inc.,
Québec)

Gouvernement du Québec – Refundable Tax Credit for Book
Publishing program – Gestion SODEC

1685 Talbot Boulevard, Québec, QC G2N 0C6
Tel.: 418-877-0259
Toll-free: 1-866-882-0091
Fax: 418-780-1716
www.pratico-pratiques.com
www.5ingredients15minutes.com

Comments and suggestions: info@pratico-pratiques.com

Prep, Freeze
and Cook *in* 5 INGREDIENTS 15 MINUTES

Prep, Freeze and Cook *in* 5 INGREDIENTS 15 MINUTES

135 weekly dinners

in 5 ingredients
15 minutes
for busy families

PRATICO
EDITION

Table of Contents

No-fuss,
Make-ahead Meals
for Busy Weeknights

We're all running short on time during the week. We all have so many different activities on the go—it can be tough to find time to make a quick meal that will satisfy everyone! Sometimes this hectic pace has us reaching for store-bought meals, which are often not very healthy.

If you're like us and want to eat well even when you're short on time, this book from the *5 Ingredients - 15 Minutes* collection is for you! You'll find tips for maximizing your time in the kitchen, and more importantly, ways to ensure you always have a delicious meal close at hand and ready to serve. The possibilities of the freezer—and everything it can store— are limitless so we rely on it for preserving our make-ahead recipes. Sauces, marinated meats and chopped vegetables, stored in freezer bags or containers, are just waiting to be reheated!

You'll find in this book a variety of meal solutions ready in no time. And the best part: the whole family will love them, guaranteed!

Say goodbye to weeknights too busy for good hearty meals!

25 Tips
for Stress-free Cooking

Housework, laundry, hockey practice, swimming lesson, workout... It's tough to find the time to cook on busy weeknights. And yet there's nothing better than a home-cooked meal to relax after a long day and enjoy some quality time with the family!

So how can you enjoy delicious dinners every night when time is so short?

A well-planned weekly menu is a good start! By planning out what you're going to eat during the week, you can get better organized, and more importantly, you can prep and/or cook a few ingredients in advance. It's also easier to plan dishes that use some of the same ingredients—a great way to save time and waste less food!

Read on to find tips for fool-proof organizing, techniques for optimal preservation and even ideas for increasing your efficiency: everything you need to make cooking stress-free!

1 Make a plan

Before you set foot in the grocery store, you should have your menu for the week in mind. What recipes will you use? What ingredients do they share? What do you already have on hand? Answer these questions first to maximize your time at the supermarket and in the kitchen!

> Keep a copy of your menu where you can see it: it'll help you remember your plans and stay efficient!

2 Double and freeze

To have a side dish always ready to go, double (or even triple!) the amount of rice, quinoa or couscous you cook. The extras will keep longer in the freezer, and you can simply reheat them in the microwave or on the stove when you're ready to eat.

3 Stay one step ahead

Take a few extra minutes when you're putting away your groceries and prep the fruits, vegetables and meats you've brought home. Cut up fresh fruits and veggies for snacks, chop the vegetables for your weekly menu and trim and marinate meats to save yourself time during the week.

4 Shredded cheese at the ready

Refrigerated or frozen in an airtight bag, pre-shredded cheese is always ready to add to gratins, fajitas, pasta and other delicious dishes!

5 We love leftovers!

When designing your menu for the week, think about what leftovers can be reused. For example, if you cook a large amount of pasta, you can transform the extra noodles into a delicious pasta salad for lunch. And cooked chicken breasts are ideal for sandwiches and stir-fries!

6 Leeks, pronto

Prepping leeks can be time-consuming, but don't let that stop you from enjoying them! Wash several at a time, and then slice them into rounds. Place them in the freezer in small freezer bags and all that's left to do is toss them into stir-fries, soups and stews whenever you feel like it!

7 Seasonings at your fingertips

Wash and trim aromatic ingredients in advance. You can divide them into the compartments of an ice tray and add a little oil, butter or water. They'll freeze into cubes ready to use on a whim. It's never been easier to add fresh herbs, garlic, lemongrass and other seasonings to your recipes!

8 Cook by night

Sear meat in the evening, then assemble the recipe in the slow-cooker before bed and let tomorrow night's dinner simmer as you sleep! The next morning, let it cool as you eat breakfast and then put it in the fridge for the day. All you'll have to do at dinnertime is reheat!

9 Pre-grated ginger

Keep minced ginger at the ready by grating it in advance. Freeze it in an ice-tray and you'll have little portions of about 15 ml (1 tbsp) ready to go–the perfect amount for making dinner for four!

Hard-boiled eggs to the rescue 10

Hard-boiled eggs are perfect for sandwiches and salads or all on their own as snacks. So why not make a few extra to save yourself some time? You can keep them, unpeeled, in the fridge for up to a week in an airtight container.

11
Rainy day recipes

A rainy Sunday is the perfect opportunity to stock your freezer. Prepare a few dishes that freeze well, like lasagna, chili or meatball stew. You'll thank yourself come busy weeknights!

13
Freeze your fruits!

Keep a supply of frozen fruit to add to smoothies, muffins, crumbles and upside-down cakes. Just wash and trim your favorite fruits and freeze them on a baking sheet first, to avoid clumping. Then you can create different mixes in airtight bags or containers for freezing.

12
Stewed solutions

Craving a delicious stew but don't have a slow cooker to let it simmer all day? Save time by cooking your stew on the stove during dinner, then refrigerating it. Your meal will be ready to enjoy the next evening, or whenever you need it.

14
Instant rice noodles

Ideal for Asian-inspired stir-fries and soups, rice noodles are a must-have pantry staple. Soak them in a bowl of water in the fridge during the day and then simply drain and add to your recipe that evening!

Don't forget about soup! # 15

It is delicious and comforting, not to mention easy to prepare—don't underestimate the power of soup for quick dinners! Slice up vegetable peels and trimmings each time you cook and keep them in a freezer bag in the freezer. They'll serve as the perfect base for a delicious vegetable soup!

16 Citrus juice

If your lemons and limes are starting to dry up or you just want to stock up on citrus juice, the solution is simple! Just squeeze the juice into an ice tray and pop it into the freezer—that way you'll always have perfect small portions of juice on hand, as each cube will give you about 15 ml (1 tbsp) of juice.

17 Slice and dice efficiently

Nothing beats having the right tools to optimize meal prep! Ideally, you should have a chef's knife (blade 20 cm or 8 in long), four to five paring knives and a serrated knife for slicing tomatoes. Don't forget to sharpen them regularly—it can increase your efficiency in the kitchen tenfold!

18 Save steps

Take out all the ingredients you need before you start cooking to maximize your time and avoid running back and forth from the fridge to the stove. You can also pull the garbage can over or toss all your scraps in a large bowl to save even more steps!

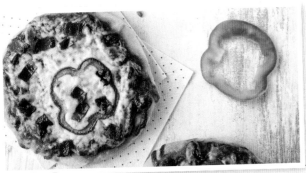

19 Get creative with leftovers recipes

On busy nights, those leftover odds and ends in the fridge can be just the ticket! Plan ahead so that you're always ready to throw together a comforting gratin or a delicious pizza with whatever's in the fridge. Grate a little hard cheese (cheddar, mozzarella, parmesan, etc.) and keep it in the freezer. Have a few frozen naan breads, frozen tortillas or a package of frozen pizza dough on hand for a quick meal the whole family will love!

21 Lifesaver ingredients

For those busy evenings, stock up on frozen fruits and vegetables, and pre-marinated meats. Herbs in tubes, shredded cheese blends and store-bought vinaigrettes are also great ways to add a ton of flavour to your meals that don't require a ton of time!

20 Operation Organization

Take the time to tidy up the kitchen. Keep your counters, cabinets, cupboards, drawers, fridge and freezer uncluttered and well-organized to stay efficient!

22 Get in microwave mode

Vegetables, fish, omelettes and even pasta can all be cooked in just a few minutes in the microwave. You just need to have enough liquid (water or stock) and use the proper containers and accessories (silicone dishes, plastic wrap, steamer bags, etc.).

23 Boiling water in no time

Heat water for pasta in the kettle while you prepare the rest of the meal—it'll boil faster than in a pot! You can then just transfer it to a pot on a hot burner before adding the pasta.

24 The right gear

A food processor, garlic press, citrus press, peeler, egg slicer, chopper and mandoline—these tools will help you stay efficient in the kitchen! Are you missing a few? Make a list and acquire these accessories as you need them. You'll see: they'll save you a ton of time!

25 Shelf life

Knowing how long different foods will keep can help you plan your meals for the week and cut down on waste! Here's a little guide to storing some common foods.

Food	Refrigerator	Freezer
Beef (steak and roasts)	3 to 5 days	6 to 12 months
Fresh herbs	4 days	1 year
Hard cheese	5 weeks	6 months
Berries (strawberries, raspberries, etc.)	3 to 4 days	1 year
Fatty fish (salmon, trout, etc.)	1 to 2 days	2 months
Lean fish (cod, tilapia, etc.)	2 to 3 days	6 months
Pork (chops, roasts)	3 to 5 days	4 to 6 months
Baked goods (breads, cakes, etc.)	7 days	3 months
Cooked meat with sauce	3 to 4 days	4 months
Chopped or cubed meat	1 to 2 days	3 to 4 months
Cooked poultry with sauce	1 to 2 days	1 to 3 months
Tofu	1 to 2 weeks	1 to 2 months

Microwave photo: Shutterstock.

Main Dishes

Chicken Teriyaki Noodle Bowl **40**

Chili con Carne **56**

Coquilles Saint-Jacques **50**

Korean Meatballs **26**

Macaroni with Meat Sauce, Spinach and Ricotta **58**

Meatballs **20**

Meatballs in Tomato Sauce **24**

Meat Sauce **52**

Meat Sauce Sloppy Joes **54**

Pulled Pork **28**

Pulled Pork Burger **30**

Pulled Pork Nachos **34**

Pulled Pork Poutine **32**

Seafood Fettuccine **48**

Seafood Lasagna **46**

Seafood Sauce **44**

Swedish Meatballs **22**

Teriyaki Chicken **36**

Teriyaki Chicken Pizza **42**

Teriyaki Chicken Wraps **38**

Side Dishes

Caramelized Onions **32**

Garlic Croutons **24**

Guacamole **34**

Light Coleslaw **54**

Lime and Cilantro Basmati Rice **26**

Mashed Sweet Potatoes **22**

Spicy Cajun Fries **30**

Sweet and Sour Salad **42**

Zucchini Ribbon Salad **48**

1 Master Recipe, 3 Meal Ideas

1 Master Recipe, 3 Meal Ideas

A quick and easy recipe is a great find. But a quick and easy recipe that can be turned into several delicious meals is even better! Before diving into our convenient recipes, read on for some tips on saving even more time in the kitchen!

By Marie-Pier Marceau

Leftovers: Our misunderstood friends

Cooked and seasoned meat, poultry and fish, extra pasta and rice, the last of the sauce... these are not our enemies! Indeed, these ingredients can be turned into unexpected delicious meals. Reinvent leftovers by getting creative with what you find in the fridge!

Getting a head start

Getting ready for a busy week by preparing a few steps of a recipe can be a lifesaver! You're wondering what type of preparation you can do in advance? Sauces and dressings, sure, but you can also cook rice, pasta and quinoa ahead of time. You can chop veggies and grate cheese one or two days before the meal, and other kinds of prep can be refrigerated or frozen for a few days or even weeks, like pie dough or pancake batter.

Make-ahead meatballs

Meatballs are delicious served in sauce or on skewers, but it's such a fuss to prepare them every time! Here's a simple solution: increase the quantities of your meatball recipe and make a bigger batch. Bake them on a baking sheet or in a frying pan. Then let the meatballs cool slightly on the counter, and refrigerate to cool completely. The last step is to freeze the meatballs on a baking sheet so they don't stick together. Once they're frozen, you can put them in freezer bags or freezer safe containers so that you always have them on hand!

Versatile ingredients

A well-stocked kitchen is the key to stress-free meal prep. Choose ingredients that can be used in different kinds of recipes:

- **In the fridge:** Keep eggs, cold meats, cooked chicken strips and mixed greens.

- **In the freezer:** Always have on hand frozen fruits and vegetables, fish fillets, filled pasta and bread.

- **In the pantry:** Stock up on canned foods (beans, tuna, etc.), pasta, broth and nuts.

Freeze in portions

Rather than freezing a dish in a single container or freezer bag, divide it up into separate portions! That way, whether you're dining solo, as a couple or with the whole family, you can take out exactly the number of portions you need. For example, if you make pulled pork, use a muffin tin to freeze separate portions that will always be ready to reheat for sandwiches, salads or Friday night nachos!

Optimal storage

If you decide to prepare a recipe a few days or even weeks in advance, make sure you store it properly. Your best bet here is the freezer. Choose containers designed to be frozen—they're marked with a snowflake—and be careful not to overfill the bag or container, since food expands as it freezes. This way you can store your recipes a few weeks longer than you could in the fridge!

Learn more about freezing on pages 62 and 182.

White bread ①
4 slices
cut into cubes

2% milk ②
80 ml (⅓ cup)

Medium ground beef ③
300 g (⅔ lb)

Ground pork ④
300 g (⅔ lb)

1 egg ⑤

ALSO NEEDED:
➤ **1 onion**
chopped

MASTER RECIPE

Meatballs

Prep time: **15 minutes** • Cook time: **10 minutes** • Serves: **4**

Preparation

In a bowl, mix the bread cubes and milk. Let soak for 5 minutes.

Add the ground meats, egg and onion. Mix until smooth.

Form 24 meatballs, using about 45 ml (3 tbsp) of the meat preparation for each one.

Heat a little olive oil in a pot over medium heat. Cook the meatballs for 10 to 12 minutes, stirring a few times, until they are cooked through. Remove from heat.

Transfer the meatballs to an airtight container. Let it cool slightly on the counter, then refrigerate to cool completely.

Place in the freezer.

PER SERVING	
Calories	543
Protein	33 g
Fat	35 g
Carbohydrates	23 g
Fibre	2 g
Iron	4 mg
Calcium	83 mg
Sodium	302 mg

Chef's Secret

Make perfect meatballs everytime

Here are three easy tips for meatballs that will hold their shape:

• Moisten your hands with water or a little oil before forming the meatballs to prevent the meat from sticking to them.

• If your meatballs have a tendency to fall apart, add breadcrumbs or some oats to the mix.

• Don't forget the egg! It's a key ingredient because it serves as the binding agent.

Meatballs
1 recipe (page 20)

Butter
45 ml (3 tbsp)

Beef stock
low sodium
375 ml (1 ½ cups)

Dijon mustard
30 ml (2 tbsp)

Cooking cream (15%)
125 ml (½ cup)

ALSO NEEDED:
➤ **Flour**
45 ml (3 tbsp)

OPTIONAL:
➤ **Oregano**
chopped
30 ml (2 tbsp)

Swedish Meatballs

Prep time: **15 minutes** • Cook time: **6 minutes** • Serves: **4**

Preparation

The night before your meal, let the meatballs thaw out in the refrigerator.

When ready to eat, melt the butter in a pot over medium heat. Sprinkle with flour and cook for 30 seconds, stirring, without letting the flour brown.

Add the stock and Dijon mustard. Bring to a boil, whisking.

Add the cream. Season with salt and pepper, and stir well. Add the meatballs and simmer for 6 to 8 minutes.

Sprinkle with oregano before serving, if desired.

PER SERVING	
Calories	717
Protein	36 g
Fat	49 g
Carbohydrates	29 g
Fibre	2 g
Iron	4 mg
Calcium	126 mg
Sodium	811 mg

Side Dish Idea

Mashed sweet potatoes

Peel 4 sweet potatoes and 1 potato and cut them into cubes. Place the cubes in a pot and cover with cold, salted water. Bring to a boil and then cook for 15 minutes, until tender. Drain and mash with 80 ml (⅓ cup) milk, 15 ml (1 tbsp) butter and 45 ml (3 tbsp) chopped parsley. Season with salt and pepper.

Meatballs ①
1 recipe (page 20)

1 onion ②
chopped

Garlic ③
minced
15 ml (1 tbsp)

Tomato sauce ④
625 ml (2 ½ cups)

Parmesan ⑤
shaved
125 ml (½ cup)

Meatballs in Tomato Sauce

Prep time: **15 minutes** • Cook time: **16 minutes** • Serves: **4**

Preparation

The night before your meal, let the meatballs thaw out in the refrigerator.

When ready to eat, heat a little olive oil in a pot over medium heat. Cook the onion and garlic for 1 minute.

Add the tomato sauce and bring to a boil. Simmer for 10 to 12 minutes, stirring often.

Add the meatballs and continue cooking for 5 to 8 minutes. Garnish with parmesan shavings before serving.

PER SERVING	
Calories	614
Protein	41 g
Fat	37 g
Carbohydrates	29 g
Fibres	4 g
Iron	5 mg
Calcium	278 mg
Sodium	1,307 mg

Side Dish Idea

Garlic croutons

In a small pot, melt 45 ml (3 tbsp) butter with 15 ml (1 tbsp) minced garlic over low heat. Cut a baguette into 12 slices and brush with the garlic butter. Place the croutons on a baking sheet. Broil for 2 minutes, until golden brown.

Korean Meatballs

Prep time: **15 minutes** • Cook time: **8 minutes** • Serves: **4**

Meatballs ❶
1 recipe (page 20)

Honey ❷
45 ml (3 tbsp)

Hoisin sauce ❸
45 ml (3 tbsp)

Soy sauce ❹
low sodium
60 ml (¼ cup)

**Coleslaw
vegetable mix** ❺
500 ml (2 cups)

Preparation

The night before your meal, let the meatballs thaw out in the refrigerator.

When ready to eat, bring the honey to a boil in a pot with the hoisin sauce, soy sauce, rice vinegar, and sriracha, if desired.

Add the meatballs and cover. Simmer for 5 to 8 minutes over low heat.

Add the coleslaw vegetable mix and stir. Cover and continue cooking for 3 to 4 minutes.

PER SERVING	
Calories	645
Protein	35 g
Fat	35 g
Carbohydrates	46 g
Fibre	3 g
Iron	6 mg
Calcium	115 mg
Sodium	1,127 mg

Side Dish Idea

Lime and cilantro basmati rice

Rinse 250 ml (1 cup) basmati rice in cold water. Place in a pot with 500 ml (2 cups) cold water, 15 ml (1 tbsp) lime zest and 1 chopped onion. Season with salt and pepper. Bring to a boil over medium heat. Cover and cook for 18 to 20 minutes over medium-low heat. When ready to serve, add 45 ml (3 tbsp) chopped cilantro.

ALSO NEEDED:
➤ **Rice vinegar**
45 ml (3 tbsp)

OPTIONAL:
➤ **Sriracha**
5 ml (1 tsp)

Chicken stock ❶
180 ml (¾ cup)

Brown sugar ❷
30 ml (2 tbsp)

Chili powder ❸
15 ml (1 tbsp)

Smoked paprika ❹
15 ml (1 tbsp)

Pork ❺
1.5 kg (3 ⅓ lb) bone-in
shoulder

ALSO NEEDED:
➤ **1 onion**
chopped

MASTER RECIPE

Pulled Pork

Prep time: **15 minutes** • Cook time on low: **7 hours** • Cook time on high: **30 minutes** • Serves: **4**

Preparation

In the slow cooker, mix the sugar, chili powder, smoked paprika and onion into the chicken stock. Season with salt and pepper.

Remove excess fat from the pork shoulder.

Place the pork shoulder into the slow cooker and turn it several times to ensure it is thoroughly coated with sauce. Cover and cook on low for 7 to 8 hours, until the meat shreds easily with a fork.

Remove the pork shoulder from the slow cooker, and shred the meat using two forks.

Return the shredded pork to the slow cooker, and cook on high for 30 minutes.

Transfer the pulled pork and cooking juices to airtight containers. Let it cool slightly on the counter, then refrigerate to cool completely. Place the containers in the freezer.

PER SERVING	
Calories	375
Protein	48 g
Fat	15 g
Carbohydrates	11 g
Fibre	2 g
Iron	4 mg
Calcium	58 mg
Sodium	393 mg

Learn More

Pulled pork

Pulled pork, a traditional dish from the southern United States, has been gaining popularity for some time now. Often served as a burger, but also found on pub menus in poutine and mac and cheese, slow-cooked pulled pork is juicy, tender and hard to resist. A perfect way to satisfy the whole family!

Pulled pork ①
1 recipe (page 28)

4 hamburger buns ②

1 avocado ③
cut into quarters

Creamy coleslaw ④
250 ml (1 cup)

BBQ sauce ⑤
125 ml (½ cup)

Pulled Pork Burger

Prep time: **15 minutes** • Cook time: **5 minutes** • Serves: **4**

Preparation

The night before your meal, let the pulled pork thaw out in the refrigerator.

When ready to eat, place the pulled pork and cooking juice in a pot. Cover and reheat over low heat for 5 to 6 minutes, stirring occasionally.

Garnish the buns with avocado slices, pulled pork, coleslaw and BBQ sauce.

PER SERVING	
Calories	715
Protein	54 g
Fat	28 g
Carbohydrates	63 g
Fibre	7 g
Iron	5 mg
Calcium	130 mg
Sodium	1,057 mg

Side Dish Idea

Spicy Cajun fries

Cut 4 or 5 potatoes (red, yellow, Russet or Idaho) into sticks. In a bowl, mix the potatoes with 30 ml (2 tbsp) olive oil, 15 ml (1 tbsp) Cajun seasoning, 1.25 ml (¼ tsp) smoked paprika and 15 ml (1 tbsp) lime zest. Spread the potatoes out in a single layer on a baking sheet lined with parchment paper. Bake for 30 minutes at 205°C (400°F).

Pulled pork ①
1 recipe (page 28)

4 to 5 yellow potatoes ②

Gravy ③
low sodium
375 ml (1 ½ cups)

Cheese curds or diced cheddar ④
200 g (about ½ lb)

Caramelized onions ⑤
180 ml (¾ cup)

ALSO NEEDED:
➤ **Olive oil**
30 ml (2 tbsp)

Pulled Pork Poutine

Prep time: **15 minutes** • Cook time: **25 minutes** • Serves: 4

Preparation

The night before your meal, let the pulled pork thaw out in the refrigerator.

When ready to eat, preheat the oven to 205°C (400°F).

Cut the potatoes into sticks.

In a bowl, mix the potatoes with the oil. Season with salt and pepper.

Spread the potatoes out in a single layer on a baking sheet lined with parchment paper. Bake for 20 to 25 minutes, until the fries are crispy.

Place the pulled pork and cooking juice in a pot. Cover and reheat over low heat for 5 to 6 minutes, stirring occasionally.

In another pot, heat the gravy over medium-low heat for a few minutes.

Divide the fries into four bowls and add pulled pork and cheese. Top with the sauce, and garnish each bowl with caramelized onions.

Homemade Version

Caramelized onions

In a large frying pan, melt 15 ml (1 tbsp) butter over medium heat. Cook 3 sliced onions for 4 to 5 minutes. Sprinkle with 30 ml (2 tbsp) sugar and continue cooking for 5 to 8 minutes, stirring regularly, until the onions are caramelized. Season with salt and pepper. Add 5 ml (1 tsp) minced thyme and 80 ml (⅓ cup) red wine. Stir and let simmer until the liquid has fully evaporated. Remove from heat and let cool.

PER SERVING	
Calories	840
Protein	65 g
Fat	39 g
Carbohydrates	57 g
Fibre	6 g
Iron	5 mg
Calcium	459 mg
Sodium	1,177 mg

Pulled pork ①
1 recipe (page 28)

Tortilla chips ②
1 bag (220 g)

1 red onion ③
chopped

BBQ sauce ④
250 ml (1 cup)

Tex-Mex shredded cheese ⑤
375 ml (1 ½ cups)

OPTIONAL:
➤ **Romaine lettuce**
sliced
250 ml (1 cup)
➤ **Ranch dressing**
125 ml (½ cup)

Pulled Pork Nachos

Prep time: **15 minutes** • Cook time: **13 minutes** • Serves: **4**

Preparation

The night before your meal, let the pulled pork thaw out in the refrigerator.

When ready to eat, preheat the oven to 205°C (400°F).

Place the pulled pork and cooking juice in a pot. Cover and reheat over low heat for 5 to 6 minutes, stirring occasionally.

Spread out the tortilla chips on a large baking sheet. Top with pulled pork, red onion, BBQ sauce and cheese. Bake for 8 to 10 minutes.

If desired, garnish with lettuce and drizzle with ranch dressing once removed from the oven.

PER SERVING	
Calories	1,023
Protein	61 g
Fat	51 g
Carbohydrates	79 g
Fibre	7 g
Iron	5 mg
Calcium	175 mg
Sodium	1,839 mg

Side Dish Idea

Guacamole

In a bowl, place 15 ml (1 tbsp) lime juice, 30 ml (2 tbsp) chopped cilantro, 1 pinch of cayenne pepper and the flesh of 2 avocados. Use a fork to mash the avocados. Add 1 diced tomato, 60 ml (¼ cup) chopped red onion and 15 ml (1 tbsp) olive oil. Season with salt and stir.

Soy sauce ①
low sodium
180 ml (¾ cup)

Brown sugar ②
60 ml (¼ cup)

Rice vinegar ③
30 ml (2 tbsp)

Chicken ④
4 skinless breasts

Ginger ⑤
minced
15 ml (1 tbsp)

ALSO NEEDED:
➤ **Garlic**
minced
15 ml (1 tbsp)

MASTER RECIPE

Teriyaki Chicken

Prep time: **15 minutes** • Cook time: **9 minutes** • Serves: **4**

Preparation

In a bowl, mix the soy sauce, brown sugar, rice vinegar and garlic. Season with pepper.

Cut the chicken breasts into pieces.

Heat a little canola oil in a frying pan over medium heat. Cook the chicken pieces for 2 minutes on each side, until the meat is no longer pink in the centre.

Add the ginger and sauce, and stir. Bring to a boil and then simmer over low heat for 5 minutes.

Remove the pan from the heat and let it cool slightly, then refrigerate to cool completely.

Transfer the chicken and sauce to an airtight container, and place the container in the freezer.

Learn More

The meaning of "teriyaki"

In Japanese cooking, the term "teriyaki" is generally used for dishes prepared with the sauce of the same name. Teriyaki sauce is a subtle blend of sweet and salty flavours created by combining ingredients like soy sauce, ginger and honey. This sauce is added to stir-fries or marinades to give a glossy sheen to grilled meats, like in this delicious chicken recipe.

PER SERVING	
Calories	244
Protein	40 g
Fat	6 g
Carbohydrates	4 g
Fibre	0 g
Iron	1 mg
Calcium	13 mg
Sodium	504 mg

Teriyaki chicken ①
1 recipe (page 36)

1 green bell pepper ②
diced

Red cabbage ③
finely chopped
500 ml (2 cups)

Tortillas ④
8 small

2 avocados ⑤
cut in thin slices

ALSO NEEDED:
➤ **1 onion**
chopped

OPTIONAL:
➤ **Cilantro**
60 ml (¼ cup)

Teriyaki Chicken Wraps

Prep time: **15 minutes** • Cook time: **4 minutes** • Serves: 4

Preparation

The night before your meal, let the teriyaki chicken thaw out in the refrigerator.

When ready to eat, heat a little canola oil in a frying pan over medium heat. Cook the bell pepper and onion for 1 to 2 minutes.

Add the chicken and reheat for 3 to 4 minutes, stirring.

Add the red cabbage. Cook for 1 minute, stirring.

Warm the tortillas for 30 seconds in the microwave.

Fill the tortillas with the chicken and vegetables preparation, avocado slices, and cilantro if desired.

5•15 Tip

Ideas for leftover tortillas

Synonym of Mexican flavours and quick meals, tortillas make it easy to please any crowd! Soft corn tortillas are delicious when prepared traditionally, but they are also incredibly adaptable to other cuisines. Those leftover tortillas in the fridge can become wraps for lunches, quick pizzas for weeknight dinners, Friday night burritos or dainty mini quiches made in a muffin tin for a Saturday morning brunch. The possibilities are infinite, and all of them are tasty!

PER SERVING	
Calories	662
Protein	49 g
Fat	29 g
Carbohydrates	51 g
Fibre	10 g
Iron	3 mg
Calcium	57 mg
Sodium	1,070 mg

Teriyaki chicken
1 recipe (page 36)

1

Stir-fry noodles
1 package (350 g)

2

Frozen diced vegetable mix
thawed and drained
1 bag (600 g)

3

Chicken stock
low sodium
125 ml (½ cup)

4

Soy sauce
low sodium
60 ml (¼ cup)

5

OPTIONAL:
➤ **Mushrooms**
sliced
1 container (227 g)

Chicken Teriyaki Noodle Bowl

Prep time: **15 minutes** • Cook time: **7 minutes** • Serves: **4**

Preparation

The night before your meal, let the teriyaki chicken thaw out in the refrigerator.

When ready to eat, cook the noodles according to the package directions. Drain.

In the same pot, heat a little canola oil over medium heat. Cook the mixed vegetables and mushrooms, if desired, for 2 to 3 minutes.

Add the teriyaki chicken, chicken stock and soy sauce. Stir. Bring to a boil, then simmer for 5 to 8 minutes over low heat.

Add the noodles. Season with pepper and stir.

PER SERVING	
Calories	666
Protein	58 g
Fat	15 g
Carbohydrates	76 g
Fibre	8 g
Iron	6 mg
Calcium	74 mg
Sodium	1,384 mg

Learn More

What is soy sauce made from?

Soy sauce originally comes from China, and is made from fermented soy beans and grains like wheat, rice or barley. Light soy sauce is the saltiest variety and is most often used in Thai cooking. There are also darker, thicker soy sauces as well as low-sodium versions. Keep in mind some soy sauces found in the grocery store are not made according to the traditional recipe. Sometimes the flavour and colour are produced artificially with additives instead of through the fermentation process. To make the best choice, we recommend checking the ingredients before checking out!

Teriyaki chicken ❶
1 recipe (page 36)

Pizza dough ❷
500 g (about 1 lb)

Thick teriyaki sauce ❸
60 ml (¼ cup)

1 green bell pepper ❹
diced

Mozzarella ❺
shredded
500 ml (2 cups)

ALSO NEEDED:
➤ **1 small red onion**
diced

Teriyaki Chicken Pizza

Prep time: **15 minutes** • Cook time: **20 minutes** • Serves: **4 (2 pizzas, 20 cm - 8 in each)**

Preparation

The night before your meal, let the teriyaki chicken thaw out in the refrigerator.

When ready to eat, preheat the oven to 205°C (400°F).

Stretch out each of the balls of dough on a floured surface and form two 20-cm (8-in) circles.

Place the dough on a baking sheet lined with parchment paper. Brush the teriyaki sauce over the dough, leaving a 1 cm (½ in) perimeter free for the crust.

Top with the teriyaki chicken, bell pepper, red onion and mozzarella. Bake for 20 to 25 minutes.

PER SERVING	
Calories	762
Protein	64 g
Fat	23 g
Carbohydrates	70 g
Fibre	3 g
Iron	5 mg
Calcium	365 mg
Sodium	1,901 mg

Side Dish Idea

Sweet and sour salad

In a salad bowl, mix 60 ml (¼ cup) sesame oil (not toasted) with 30 ml (2 tbsp) lime juice, 15 ml (1 tbsp) honey and 15 ml (1 tbsp) sesame seeds. Add 250 ml (1 cup) bean sprouts, 250 ml (1 cup) broccoli cut in small florets and 1 carrot cut in thin julienne strips. Season with salt and pepper, and stir well.

**Mixed frozen shrimp
and scallops**
thawed
1 bag (340 g)

1

Vegetable stock
375 ml (1 ½ cups)

2

Shallots
125 ml (½ cup)

3

White wine
60 ml (¼ cup)

4

Cooking cream (15%)
125 ml (½ cup)

5

ALSO NEEDED:
➤ **Butter**
45 ml (3 tbsp)
➤ **Flour**
30 ml (2 tbsp)

OPTIONAL:
➤ **Dill**
chopped
60 ml (¼ cup)

MASTER RECIPE

Seafood Sauce

Prep time: **15 minutes** • Cook time: **10 minutes** • Serves: **4**

Preparation

Place the seafood and vegetable stock in a pot, and bring to a boil. Drain the seafood over a bowl in order to keep the stock. Place the seafood on a plate.

In the same pot, melt the butter over medium heat. Cook the shallots for 2 minutes.

Sprinkle with flour and stir. Pour in the filtered stock, white wine and cream. Bring to a boil, stirring.

Add the seafood and the dill, if desired. Season with salt and pepper and stir well.

Remove from the heat and let cool slightly on the counter, then refrigerate to cool completely.

Transfer the seafood sauce to an airtight container. Place the container in the freezer.

PER SERVING	
Calories	222
Protein	13 g
Fat	14 g
Carbohydrates	10 g
Fibre	1 g
Iron	1 mg
Calcium	60 mg
Sodium	783 mg

5•15 Tip

Buy mixed frozen seafood

When every minute counts, choose frozen seafood! A shrimps and scallops mix is a quick and easy solution for tasty meals that can be put together quickly: pasta, pizza, gratins, even Coquilles Saint-Jacques. Before cooking, thaw them out in the fridge or in cold water, and then pat dry with a paper towel. Enjoy your favourite seafood delicacies in no time at all!

Seafood sauce ❶
1 recipe (page 44)

12 fresh lasagna sheets ❷

Cream cheese ❸
softened
1 container (250 g)

Basil ❹
chopped
60 ml (¼ cup)

Mozzarella ❺
shredded
500 ml (2 cups)

Seafood Lasagna

Prep time: **15 minutes** • Cook time: **30 minutes** • Serves: **6**

Preparation

The night before your meal, let the seafood sauce thaw out in the refrigerator.

When ready to cook, preheat the oven to 205°C (400°F).

Cook the noodles *al dente* in a pot of boiling, salted water. Drain.

While the noodles are cooking, mix the seafood sauce and cream cheese in another pot and bring to a boil.

Add the basil to the sauce and stir.

Pour a little of the seafood sauce into a square baking dish. Place three lasagna sheets side by side in the dish. Cover with a third of the sauce and top with three more noodles. Repeat two more times to form four layers in total. Cover with mozzarella.

Cover the dish with a sheet of aluminum foil. Bake for 10 to 15 minutes.

Remove the aluminum foil and continue baking for 15 minutes.

PER SERVING	
Calories	756
Protein	29 g
Fat	36 g
Carbohydrates	77 g
Fibre	4 g
Iron	2 mg
Calcium	336 mg
Sodium	984 mg

Healthy Choice

This lasagna is an excellent source of calcium

In addition to being a source of protein and fibre, a serving of this seafood lasagna provides around 30% of the recommended daily intake of calcium for an adult aged 19 to 50. This essential mineral helps maintain good bone health and prevent osteoporosis.

Seafood sauce ❶
1 recipe (page 44)

Fettuccine ❷
350 g (about ¾ lb)

Salmon ❸
fillets
300 g (⅔ lb)
skin removed
and cut into small cubes

Basil ❹
chopped
60 ml (¼ cup)

Brie cheese ❺
150 g (⅓ lb)
cut into cubes

Seafood Fettuccine

Prep time: **15 minutes** • Cook time: **10 minutes** • Serves: 4

Preparation

The night before your meal, let the seafood sauce thaw out in the refrigerator.

When ready to eat, cook the fettuccine *al dente* in a pot of boiling, salted water. Drain.

While the pasta is cooking, bring the seafood sauce to a boil in another pot over medium-low heat.

Add the salmon and basil to the seafood sauce. Stir and cook for 3 to 4 minutes.

Add the pasta and Brie to the pot. Continue cooking for 1 minute, stirring.

PER SERVING	
Calories	816
Protein	46 g
Fat	36 g
Carbohydrates	74 g
Fibre	4 g
Iron	4 mg
Calcium	161 mg
Sodium	1,243 mg

Side Dish Idea

Zucchini ribbon salad

Using a mandolin slicer or a vegetable peeler, cut 1 green zucchini and 1 yellow zucchini lengthwise into thin ribbons. Spread the zucchini ribbons on a baking sheet lined with parchment paper. Drizzle with olive oil and bake for 3 to 4 minutes at 190°C (375°F). In a salad bowl, mix 60 ml (¼ cup) balsamic vinegar with ½ thinly sliced red onion and 30 ml (2 tbsp) chopped parsley. Add the zucchini ribbons and toss gently. Season with salt and pepper.

Seafood sauce ❶
1 recipe (page 44)

6 potatoes ❷
peeled and cut
into cubes

8 mushrooms ❸
chopped

Swiss cheese ❹
shredded
250 ml (1 cup)

Panko bread crumbs ❺
60 ml (¼ cup)

ALSO NEEDED:
➤ **2% milk**
warm
60 ml (¼ cup)
➤ **Butter**
30 ml (2 tbsp)

Coquilles Saint-Jacques

Prep time: **15 minutes** • Cook time: **22 minutes** • Serves: **4**

Preparation

The night before your meal, let the seafood sauce thaw out in the refrigerator.

When ready to cook, preheat the oven to 205°C (400°F).

Place the potatoes in a pot, cover with cold water and season with salt. Bring to a boil and simmer for 18 to 20 minutes, until tender. Drain.

Mash the potatoes with the warm milk and butter. Season with salt and pepper.

In another pot, heat the seafood sauce with the mushrooms over medium heat for 2 to 3 minutes.

Fill a pastry bag fitted with a star tip with the mashed potatoes. Pipe the potatoes along the edges of four Coquilles Saint-Jacques dishes.

Spoon the seafood sauce into the centre of each dish, cover with cheese and then sprinkle with the panko breadcrumbs.

Bake for 11 to 14 minutes.

Broil for 1 minute.

PER SERVING	
Calories	540
Protein	26 g
Fat	29 g
Carbohydrates	46 g
Fibre	4 g
Iron	2 mg
Calcium	327 mg
Sodium	873 mg

Learn More

The origins of Coquilles Saint-Jacques

Coquilles Saint-Jacques takes its name from a practice of the pilgrims in the Middle Ages who would travel the Camino de Santiago to the shrine of Saint James (Saint-Jacques) in Santiago de Compostela: upon reaching their destination in the north of Spain, they would gather scallop shells (*coquilles*) on the beaches to hang on their clothes for good luck.

Lean ground beef ❶
450 g (1 lb)

Frozen diced ❷
vegetable mix
375 ml (1 ½ cups)

Marinara sauce ❸
500 ml (2 cups)

Tomato paste ❹
45 ml (3 tbsp)

Italian seasoning ❺
15 ml (1 tbsp)

ALSO NEEDED:
➤ **Garlic**
minced
15 ml (1 tbsp)

MASTER RECIPE

Meat Sauce

Prep time: **15 minutes** • Cook time: **16 minutes** • Serves: 4

Preparation

Heat a little olive oil in a pot over medium heat. Cook the ground beef for 4 to 5 minutes, breaking up the meat with a wooden spoon.

Add the vegetables and garlic. Stir and cook for 2 minutes.

Add the marinara sauce, tomato paste and Italian seasoning. Season with salt and pepper.

Bring to a boil, then simmer over medium-low heat for 10 to 12 minutes.

Remove the pot from the heat and let it cool slightly on the counter, then refrigerate to cool completely.

Transfer the meat sauce to an airtight container. Place the container in the freezer.

PER SERVING	
Calories	433
Protein	25 g
Fat	25 g
Carbohydrates	26 g
Fibre	5 g
Iron	4 mg
Calcium	77 mg
Sodium	708 mg

Mix It Up

Change up the ingredients!

Want to change things a bit to reinvent this sauce? Why not replace the meat (or just a portion of it) with pork, lentils or crumbled tofu? The same goes for the seasoning: try it with your favourite spices, or give it a little kick by adding Sriracha sauce or cayenne pepper. Don't be afraid to get creative!

Meat sauce ❶
1 recipe (page 52)

Chili sauce ❷
60 ml (¼ cup)

Worcestershire sauce ❸
30 ml (2 tbsp)

4 hamburger buns ❹

Orange cheddar ❺
shredded
250 ml (1 cup)

Meat Sauce Sloppy Joes

Prep time: **15 minutes** • Cook time: **8 minutes** • Serves: **4**

Preparation

The night before your meal, let the meat sauce thaw out in the refrigerator.

When ready to eat, reheat the meat sauce with the chili sauce and Worcestershire sauce in a pot for 8 to 10 minutes, until thickened.

Slice the buns in half widthwise.

Melt a little butter in a frying pan over medium heat. Toast the inside of the buns for 30 seconds to 1 minute.

Fill the buns with the meat sauce and shredded cheese.

PER SERVING	
Calories	694
Protein	35 g
Fat	34 g
Carbohydrates	60 g
Fibre	7 g
Iron	6 mg
Calcium	289 mg
Sodium	1,440 mg

Side Dish Idea

Light coleslaw

In a salad bowl, mix 180 ml (¾ cup) plain yogurt with 15 ml (1 tbsp) honey, 60 ml (¼ cup) chopped parsley, 5 ml (1 tsp) garlic powder, 15 ml (1 tbsp) apple cider vinegar and 5 ml (1 tsp) curry powder. Season with salt and pepper. Add 750 ml (3 cups) coleslaw vegetable mix and stir.

Meat sauce ①
1 recipe (page 52)

Chili seasoning mix ②
1 pouch (39 g)

4 Italian tomatoes ③
diced

Kidney beans ④
rinsed and drained
1 can (540 ml)

3 green onions ⑤
chopped

OPTIONAL:
➤ **Sour cream (14%)**
125 ml (½ cup)

➤ **Tex-Mex
shredded cheese**
125 ml (½ cup)

Chili con Carne

Prep time: **15 minutes** • Cook time: **8 minutes** • Serves: **4**

Preparation

The night before your meal, let the meat sauce thaw out in the refrigerator.

When ready to eat, reheat the sauce with the chili seasoning mix, tomatoes and kidney beans in a pot over medium-low heat for 8 to 10 minutes.

Divide chili into bowls, and top with sour cream and shredded cheese, if desired. Sprinkle with green onion.

PER SERVING	
Calories	691
Protein	39 g
Fat	34 g
Carbohydrates	58 g
Fibre	14 g
Iron	7 mg
Calcium	162 mg
Sodium	1,596 mg

Healthy Choice

Vegetarian Chili

Originally a Mexican dish that has become very popular in Tex-Mex cuisine, chili features ground beef with a mix of spices: dried ground chili peppers, pepper, cumin, oregano, paprika, garlic and cloves. You can put a vegetarian spin on this formula and make *chili sin carne* by choosing a meatless or tofu-based sauce. A great way to cut down on your meat consumption!

Meat sauce ❶
1 recipe (page 52)

Macaroni ❷
750 ml (3 cups)

Spinach ❸
trimmed
500 ml (2 cups)

Ricotta ❹
180 ml (¾ cup)

Parmesan ❺
grated
60 ml (¼ cup)

OPTIONAL:
➤ **Parsley**
chopped
60 ml (¼ cup)

Macaroni with Meat Sauce, Spinach and Ricotta

Prep time: **15 minutes** • Cook time: **10 minutes** • Serves: **4**

Preparation

The night before your meal, let the meat sauce thaw in the refrigerator.

When ready to eat, bring a pot of salted water to a boil and cook the macaroni *al dente*. Drain.

While the pasta is boiling, bring the meat sauce to a boil in another pot over medium heat.

Add the macaroni, spinach, and parsley, if desired. Reheat for 1 minute, stirring.

Serve the macaroni in bowls and garnish with ricotta and parmesan.

5•15 Tip

Adapt the recipe for the freezer

Lasagna, cannelloni and macaroni with meat sauce all freeze easily and make great lunches. If you are planning to freeze your dish, add a little more sauce than usual—when you reheat the dish in the oven, some sauce will be absorbed by the pasta.

PER SERVING	
Calories	857
Protein	44 g
Fat	35 g
Carbohydrates	90 g
Fibre	8 g
Iron	6 mg
Calcium	282 mg
Sodium	866 mg

Main Dishes

Apple and Sweet Potato Pork Chops **102**

Apple Jelly Chicken Wings **124**

Asian-style Pork and Vegetable Stir-fry **176**

Asparagus Chicken en Papillote **138**

Balsamic Pork Tenderloin **108**

BBQ Beef and Vegetable Skewers **120**

BBQ Pork Tenderloin **84**

BBQ Pulled Chicken **96**

Beef Kebabs **136**

Beef, Mango and Pepper Stir-fry **160**

Beef Stroganoff **66**

Bell Pepper Beef **86**

Butter Beef Stir-fry **152**

Cajun Sausages **68**

Chicken and Broccoli Casserole **88**

Chicken and Broccoli Rice Casserole **132**

Chicken and Thai Basil Stir-fry **164**

Chickpea and Chorizo Stew **100**

Chinese-style Beef and Broccoli **76**

Coconut Ginger Mahi-mahi **82**

Cod Curry **90**

Creamy Tomato Chicken **110**

Fajita-style Salmon **106**

General Tso-style Drumsticks **64**

Ham and Cheddar Frittata **118**

Hawaiian Chicken **80**

Honey Mustard Pork **94**

Honey Sesame Chicken **144**

Mango Curry Chicken **178**

Maple BBQ Pork Chops **78**

Maple Chicken and Bell Pepper Stir-fry **156**

Maple-glazed Chicken **104**

One Pan Honey Ginger Tofu **114**

One Pan Salmon, Edamame and Vegetables **126**

One pan Sausages and Apples **134**

One Pan Shrimp and Pancetta **122**

Orange and Asparagus Chicken Stir-fry **170**

Orange Rosemary Glazed Salmon **140**

Orange Tofu Stir-fry **154**

Peanut Pork Stir-fry **146**

Pineapple-glazed Shrimp **148**

Pork and Vegetable Fried Rice **168**

Pork Gyros **128**

Port Veal Stew **92**

Pot Roast with Vegetables **98**

Ranch Pork Chops **142**

Red Curry Chicken **150**

Red Wine Braised Beef **112**

Salmon and Mushroom Stew **70**

Salmon and Vegetable Curry **172**

Salsa Chicken **72**

Seafood Stir-fry **162**

Shrimp and Brussels Sprout Stir-fry **166**

Smoked Paprika Chicken Legs **116**

Spicy Cod and Bell Peppers **130**

Teriyaki Tofu Stir-fry **174**

Tomato and Paprika Sausages **158**

Vegetarian Chili **74**

Side Dishes

Almond Milk Rice **148**

Asian Stir-fry Sauce **164**

Chapati Bread **150**

Couscous with Herbs **140**

Egg Noodles with Chives and Butter **116**

Green and Yellow Beans with Orange **114**

Green and Yellow Beans with Pine Nuts **138**

Herbed Basmati Rice **68**

Herb Potatoes **94**

Herbs and Pine Nuts Tagliatelle **92**

Honey Mustard Vinaigrette **126**

Lemon Ginger Sauce **160**

Lemon Rice **90**

Light Fries with Paprika **124**

Lime and Cilantro Sour Cream **74**

Lime and Poppy Seed Coleslaw **108**

Mango Sauce **178**

Peanut Sauce **146**

Pear and Radish Coleslaw **84**

Rice Pilaf **156**

Roasted Asparagus and Almonds **120**

Sautéed Snow Peas with Ginger **112**

Sesame Stir-fried Rice Noodles **162**

Spicy Sour Cream **106**

Spicy Tomato Sauce **136**

Sun-dried Tomato Pesto **110**

Teriyaki Sauce **174**

Thyme Sugar Snap Peas **158**

Tzatziki **128**

Vegetable Couscous **152**

Zucchini Rice Noodles **170**

Freezer
Bags

Freezer Bags

Freezer bags are extremely useful, especially when you have a busy schedule. Learn how to use them to freeze great make-ahead meals with these helpful hints!

Par Marie-Pier Marceau

Make-ahead recipes for freezer bags are popular mostly because they're easy. It's simply a matter of preparing the ingredients, placing them in a freezer bag and adding spices and sauce!

Small, medium or large?

There are different sizes of freezer bags to choose from according to your needs. For example, if you want to freeze an entire recipe to be thawed all at once, large bags are quite useful. But if the dish is meant to be eaten in smaller portions, smaller bags are your best bet. Refreezing food that you've already thawed out is not recommended, so choose a size that allows you to take out only what you need!

Not just any bag!

Make sure you're using bags that were designed for the freezer. First indication is on the box—it should state that the bag's plastic can stand up to freezing temperatures. You should also check that the bags have airtight seals, otherwise there is a risk your food will get freezer burn.

What about thawing?

Before cooking the contents of a bag, you must let it thaw out completely. Why? To ensure meat is not kept for too long at a temperature that encourages the growth of bacteria, as well as to reduce the cooking time and ensure your meal cooks evenly! Place frozen bags in the refrigerator to thaw at least overnight before transferring the contents to the slow cooker, pot, baking dish or frying pan.

What can I freeze?

Raw and cooked food, entire recipes, prepared ingredients. . . If it can be frozen, you can put it in a freezer bag! If you're freezing cooked meat or fish, first wrap it individually in two layers of plastic wrap for optimal conservation. This prevents freezer burn and also allows you to thaw out just the portions you need. Be careful with more "fragile" foods like berries–they're best frozen first on a flat surface (like a baking sheet) or in a rigid container.

Removing air

Once you have filled the freezer bag, it's important to remove any air from it. To do so, seal the bag almost completely, leaving just enough space to insert a straw. Then suck on the straw–careful not to inhale the food!– until there is no air left in the bag. This helps preserve the taste, smell and appearance of the food.

Pro tip

If you buy ground meat in large quantities, freeze the extra meat in a large freezer bag. Remove the air from the bag and flatten it. You can then use a wooden chopstick to trace separations in the meat. When it comes time to use the meat, you'll be able to simply break off the portions you need!

Berries photo: Shutterstock

Soy sauce
low sodium
60 ml (¼ cup) **1**

Spicy Thai chili sauce **2**
125 ml (½ cup)

Rice vinegar **3**
30 ml (2 tbsp)

Ginger **4**
minced
15 ml (1 tbsp)

Chicken **5**
12 drumsticks

ALSO NEEDED:
➤ **Garlic**
minced
15 ml (1 tbsp)
➤ **Cornstarch**
30 ml (2 tbsp)

OPTIONAL:
➤ **Cilantro**
45 ml (3 tbsp)

General Tso-style Drumsticks

Prep time: **15 minutes** • Cook time on low: **5 hours** • Cook time on high: **10 minutes**
Serves: **4**

Preparation

Place the soy sauce, spicy Thai chili sauce, rice vinegar, ginger and garlic in a large freezer bag. Season with salt and pepper. Shake to mix.

Add the drumsticks and close the bag. Shake until the drumsticks are fully coated with the sauce. Remove the air from the bag and seal it.

Place the bag flat in the freezer.

The night before your meal, let the bag thaw out in the refrigerator.

When ready to cook, transfer the content of the bag to the slow cooker. Cover and cook on low for 5 to 6 hours.

Dissolve the cornstarch in a little cold water. Add to the slow cooker and stir. Cover and continue cooking for 10 minutes on high.

Garnish the drumsticks with cilantro leaves before serving, if desired.

PER SERVING	
Calories	408
Protein	40 g
Fat	19 g
Carbohydrates	15 g
Fibre	0 g
Iron	2 mg
Calcium	26 mg
Sodium	1,530 mg

Learn More

The origins of General Tso

The recipe for these chicken drumsticks is based on the famous General Tso chicken. This super popular Chinese dish was created by Taiwanese chef Peng Chang-kuei, who was inspired by traditional spicy and sour flavours. After immigrating to the United States, he had the idea to add sugar to the recipe so that it would be more appealing to the North American palate. He named his dish after General Tso, a 19th century Chinese war hero.

Beef stock
250 ml (1 cup) **1**

Red wine
180 ml (¾ cup) **2**

Dijon mustard
30 ml (2 tbsp) **3**

Beef **4**
sirloin,
750 g (about 1 ⅔ lb)
cut in strips

Mushrooms **5**
chopped
450 g (1 lb)

Beef Stroganoff

Prep time: **15 minutes** • Cook time on low: **4 hours and 10 minutes** • Serves: **4**

Preparation

In a large freezer bag, place the beef stock, wine and Dijon mustard and shake to mix.

Add the beef, mushrooms, onion and garlic. Close the bag and shake to mix. Remove the air from the bag and seal it.

Place the bag flat in the freezer.

The night before your meal, let the bag thaw out in the refrigerator.

When ready to cook, transfer the content of the bag to the slow cooker. Cover and cook on low for 4 hours.

Add the yogurt, if desired. Continue cooking for another 10 minutes.

Sprinkle with parsley before serving, if desired.

PER SERVING	
Calories	406
Protein	49 g
Fat	14 g
Carbohydrates	12 g
Fibre	2 g
Iron	5 mg
Calcium	118 mg
Sodium	459 mg

Learn More

Beef Stroganoff

Beef Stroganoff owes its name to a Russian aristocratic family, the Stroganovs. The traditional recipe was adapted by a French chef, among others, who added crème fraiche to it. Since its creation in the 19th century, this classic Russian dish has travelled all over the world, spawning many variations, some even enhanced with paprika, but always starting with a base of beef and mushrooms. Try Beef Stroganoff in the Russian style with sautéed potatoes and pickles, or serve it on a bed of fresh pasta. This quick dish is worth discovering!

ALSO NEEDED:
➤ **1 onion**
chopped
➤ **Garlic**
2 cloves
minced

OPTIONAL:
➤ **Plain yogurt (0%)**
180 ml (¾ cup)
➤ **Parsley**
chopped
30 ml (2 tbsp)

Diced tomatoes ❶
1 can (540 ml)

Chicken stock ❷
low sodium
125 ml (½ cup)

Cajun seasoning ❸
30 ml (2 tbsp)

3 bell peppers ❹
various colours
cut into pieces

8 mild Italian sausages ❺
cut into pieces

ALSO NEEDED:
➤ **1 red onion**
chopped

➤ **Garlic**
minced
15 ml (1 tbsp)

Cajun Sausages

Prep time: **15 minutes** • Cook time on low: **5 hours** • Serves: **4**

Preparation

In a bowl, mix the diced tomatoes, chicken stock, Cajun seasoning, bell peppers, sausages, red onion and garlic. Season with salt and pepper.

Transfer to a large freezer bag. Remove the air from the bag and seal it.

Place the bag flat in the freezer.

The night before your meal, let the bag thaw out in the refrigerator.

When ready to cook, transfer the content of the bag to the slow cooker. Cover and cook on low for 5 to 6 hours.

PER SERVING	
Calories	441
Protein	23 g
Fat	30 g
Carbohydrates	21 g
Fibre	3 g
Iron	2 mg
Calcium	65 mg
Sodium	1,434 mg

Side Dish

Herbed basmati rice

Rinse 250 ml (1 cup) basmati rice in cold water. Place in a pot with 500 ml (2 cups) chicken stock and 15 ml (1 tbsp) chicken seasoning. Cover and bring to a boil over medium heat. Simmer over medium-low heat for 18 to 20 minutes. Add 30 ml (2 tbsp) chopped chives and 30 ml (2 tbsp) chopped cilantro. Season with salt and pepper, and stir well.

Salmon
fillets
2.5 cm (1 in) thick
750 g (about 1 ⅔ lb)
skin removed

1

Condensed cream of mushroom
1 can (284 ml)

2

Cooking cream (15%)
125 ml (½ cup)

3

Mushrooms
chopped
1 container (227 g)

4

Cheddar
shredded
375 ml (1 ½ cup)

5

ALSO NEEDED:
➤ **Vegetable stock**
125 ml (½ cup)

➤ **1 onion**
chopped

OPTIONAL:
➤ **Lemon zest**
15 ml (1 tbsp)

➤ **Chives**
chopped
30 ml (2 tbsp)

Salmon and Mushroom Stew

Prep time: **15 minutes** • Cook time on low: **2 hours** • Serves: **4**

Preparation

Cut the salmon into large pieces.

In a large freezer bag, place the cream of mushroom, cooking cream, mushrooms, vegetable stock and onion. Season with salt and pepper, and shake to mix.

Add the pieces of salmon and close the bag. Shake until the salmon is fully coated with sauce. Remove the air from the bag and seal it.

Place the bag flat in the freezer.

The night before your meal, let the bag thaw out in the refrigerator.

When ready to cook, transfer the content of the bag to the slow cooker. Cover and cook on low for 1 hour and 50 minutes to 2 hours and 20 minutes.

In a bowl, mix the cheddar, lemon zest and chives, if desired.

Sprinkle the cheese preparation over the salmon. Cover and continue cooking for 10 minutes.

PER SERVING	
Calories	722
Protein	53 g
Fat	51 g
Carbohydrates	12 g
Fibre	2 g
Iron	2 mg
Calcium	371 mg
Sodium	984 mg

Learn More

Salmon: a valuable ally for a healthy lifestyle

Salmon has many virtues. It's an excellent source of vitamin D (37% DV) and phosphorus (26% DV), which are essential for good bone mineralization. Salmon is also high in protein which is why it's so satisfying. Even though it's a fatty fish, salmon can help you maintain good cardiovascular health because it's rich in omega-3 fatty acids. The same goes for smoked salmon. However, given its higher sodium content, smoked salmon should be consumed in moderation.

Mild salsa ❶
500 ml (2 cups)

Black beans ❷
rinsed and drained
1 can (540 ml)

Corn kernels ❸
frozen
500 ml (2 cups)

Taco seasoning ❹
low sodium
1 package (35 g)

Chicken ❺
4 skinless breasts

Salsa Chicken

Prep time: **15 minutes** • Cook time on low: **7 hours** • Serves: **4**

Preparation

In a large bowl, mix the salsa, beans, corn, taco seasoning and chicken breasts.

Transfer to a large freezer bag. Remove the air from the bag and seal it.

Place the bag flat in the freezer.

The night before your meal, let the bag thaw out in the refrigerator.

When ready to cook, transfer the content of the bag to the slow cooker. Cover and cook on low for 7 to 8 hours.

Learn More

Salsa

The Spanish word *salsa* means "sauce" and generally refers to a mix of tomatoes, onions and peppers with a variety of aromatic herbs, like cilantro, and seasonings such as spices, garlic or lime juice. Some varieties even include fruits like diced mango or pineapple. The most well-known type is the Mexican *salsa roja* served with nachos, enchiladas, burritos and other dishes.

PER SERVING	
Calories	496
Protein	55 g
Fat	4 g
Carbohydrates	62 g
Fibre	13 g
Iron	7 mg
Calcium	121 mg
Sodium	1,387 mg

Whole tomatoes ❶
1 can (796 ml)

Tomato paste ❷
60 ml (¼ cup)

Frozen diced vegetable mix ❸
1 bag (750 g)

Corn kernels ❹
250 ml (1 cup)

Mixed beans ❺
rinsed and drained
1 can (540 ml)

ALSO NEEDED:
➤ **Chili seasoning**
30 ml (2 tbsp)
➤ **Sugar**
45 ml (3 tbsp)

OPTIONAL:
➤ **Garlic**
minced
15 ml (1 tbsp)
➤ **4 tortillas**

Vegetarian Chili

Prep time: **15 minutes** • Cook time on low: **5 hours** • Serves: **4**

Preparation

Place the whole tomatoes, tomato paste, chili seasoning and sugar in a large freezer bag. Shake to mix.

Add the mixed vegetables, corn, beans, and garlic, if desired. Close the bag and shake to mix. Remove the air from the bag and seal it.

Place the bag flat in the freezer.

The night before your meal, let the bag thaw out in the refrigerator.

When ready to cook, transfer the content of the bag to the slow cooker. Season with salt and pepper. Cover and cook on low for 5 to 6 hours.

Serve the chili on tortillas, if desired.

PER SERVING	
Calories	424
Protein	17 g
Fat	5 g
Carbohydrates	83 g
Fibre	16 g
Iron	5 mg
Calcium	173 mg
Sodium	1,478 mg

Side Dish Idea

Lime and cilantro sour cream

In a bowl, mix 160 ml (⅔ cup) sour cream, 15 ml (1 tbsp) lime juice, 15 ml (1 tbsp) lime zest and 15 ml (1 tbsp) chopped cilantro. Season with salt and pepper.

Beef consommé ❶
1 can (284 ml)

Soy sauce ❷
low sodium
60 ml (¼ cup)

Brown sugar ❸
125 ml (½ cup)

Beef ❹
top sirloin
900 g (2 lb)
cut into thick strips

Broccoli ❺
1 stalk
cut into florets

ALSO NEEDED:
➤ **Ginger**
minced
15 ml (1 tbsp)

➤ **Garlic**
minced
15 ml (1 tbsp)

OPTIONAL:
➤ **Sesame oil**
(not toasted)
30 ml (2 tbsp)

Chinese-style Beef and Broccoli

Prep time: **15 minutes** • Cook time on low: **7 hours** • Serves: **8**

Preparation

Place the beef consommé, soy sauce, brown sugar, ginger, garlic, and sesame oil, if desired, in a large freezer bag. Season with salt and pepper. Shake to mix.

Add the beef and close the bag. Shake until the meat is fully coated with the sauce. Remove the air from the bag and seal it.

Place the broccoli in another large airtight bag. Remove the air from the bag and seal it.

Place the bags flat in the freezer.

The night before your meal, let the bags thaw out in the refrigerator.

When ready to cook, transfer the beef preparation to the slow cooker. Cover and cook on low for 6 hours and 30 minutes to 7 hours and 30 minutes.

Add the broccoli to the slow cooker. Cover and continue cooking for 30 minutes on low.

PER SERVING	
Calories	230
Protein	27 g
Fat	8 g
Carbohydrates	11 g
Fibre	0 g
Iron	3 mg
Calcium	23 mg
Sodium	584 mg

Healthy Choice

Broccoli

Like other cruciferous vegetables, broccoli is a champion of cancer prevention. This excellent source of vitamin C and potassium is also a good source of folic acid and contains antioxidants, vitamin A, magnesium, iron and phosphorus.

Ketchup ❶
310 ml (1 ¼ cups)

Brown sugar ❷
45 ml (3 tbsp)

Apple cider vinegar ❸
30 ml (2 tbsp)

Dry mustard ❹
15 ml (1 tbsp)

Pork ❺
4 bone-in chops
180 g (about ⅓ lb) each

ALSO NEEDED:
➤ **Chicken stock**
no salt added
250 ml (1 cup)

➤ **Maple syrup**
80 ml (⅓ cup)

OPTIONAL:
➤ **Smoked paprika**
5 ml (1 tsp)

Maple BBQ Pork Chops

Prep time: **15 minutes** • Cook time on low: **6 hours and 30 minutes** • Serves: **4**

Preparation

Place the ketchup, brown sugar, vinegar, dry mustard, chicken stock, maple syrup, and paprika, if desired, in a larger freezer bag. Shake to mix.

Remove excess fat from the pork chops.

Add the pork chops to the bag and close it. Shake until the pork chops are fully coated with the sauce. Remove the air from the bag and seal it.

Place the bag flat in the freezer.

The night before your meal, let the bag thaw out in the refrigerator.

When ready to cook, transfer the content of the bag to the slow cooker. Cover and cook on low for 6 hours and 30 minutes to 7 hours and 30 minutes.

PER SERVING	
Calories	342
Protein	28 g
Fat	6 g
Carbohydrates	46 g
Fibre	2 g
Iron	2 mg
Calcium	79 mg
Sodium	966 mg

Chef's Secret

Use cornstarch as a thickening agent

Cornstarch (also known as corn flour) has gelling properties that give volume to sauces and desserts. You can use it in this recipe to thicken the sauce. To do so, thin 15 ml (1 tbsp) cornstarch in a bit of cold water (to prevent lumps). At the end of the cook time, pour the cornstarch mixture into the slow cooker and stir until the liquid thickens. Cover and continue cooking for 30 minutes.

Pineapple chunks ①
drained
1 can (398 ml)

Brown sugar ②
45 ml (3 tbsp)

Soy sauce ③
low sodium
60 ml (¼ cup)

1 red bell pepper ④
diced

Chicken ⑤
12 boneless thighs

ALSO NEEDED:
➤ **½ red onion**
diced

Hawaiian Chicken

Prep time: **15 minutes** • Cook time on low: **5 hours** • Serves: **4**

Preparation

Place the pineapple chunks, brown sugar, soy sauce, bell pepper, chicken thighs and red onion in a large freezer bag. Season with salt and pepper. Close the bag and shake to mix. Remove the air from the bag and seal it.

Place the bag flat in the freezer.

The night before your meal, let the bag thaw out in the refrigerator.

When ready to cook, transfer the content of the bag to the slow cooker. Cover and cook on low for 5 to 6 hours.

Healthy Choice

Pineapple, a fruit bursting with nutrients!

The sweet taste of a pineapple will transport you straight to sunny Hawaii, and it's good for you too! Pineapple is an excellent source of magnesium and vitamin C and is also said to have strong antioxidant properties. There is no shortage of good reasons to serve up this exotic fruit!

PER SERVING	
Calories	397
Protein	52 g
Fat	11 g
Carbohydrates	22 g
Fibre	2 g
Iron	3 mg
Calcium	45 mg
Sodium	825 mg

Coconut milk ①
1 can (400 ml)

Ginger ②
minced
15 ml (1 tbsp)

Mahi-mahi ③
4 fillets
2.5 cm (1 in) thick

Shallots ④
chopped
60 ml (¼ cup)

Dill ⑤
chopped
30 ml (2 tbsp)

ALSO NEEDED:
➤ **Garlic**
minced
10 ml (2 tsp)

OPTIONAL:
➤ **Parsley**
chopped
30 ml (2 tbsp)

Coconut Ginger Mahi-mahi

Prep time: **15 minutes** • Cook time on low: **1 hour** • Serves: **4**

Preparation

In a large freezer bag, place the coconut milk, ginger and garlic. Season with salt and pepper, and shake to mix.

Add the mahi-mahi fillets, shallots, dill, and parsley if desired. Close the bag and shake to mix. Remove the air from the bag and seal it.

Place the bag flat in the freezer.

The night before your meal, let the bag thaw out in the refrigerator.

When ready to cook, transfer the content of the bag to the slow cooker. Cover and cook on low for 1 hour to 1 hour and 15 minutes.

PER SERVING	
Calories	311
Protein	33 g
Fat	17 g
Carbohydrates	6 g
Fibre	1 g
Iron	3 mg
Calcium	82 mg
Sodium	193 mg

5•15 Tip

Which type of fish should you choose?

Fishes with firm flesh, like mahi-mahi, haddock, halibut, cod or snapper, are best for slow cooker dishes. They absorb part of the aromatic stock as they cook, which helps them become tender and flavourful! Fishes with softer flesh, on the other hand, like sole, would turn into mush in the slow cooker.

Pork
1
1 tenderloin
675 g (about 1 ½ lb)

Brown sugar
2
125 ml (½ cup)

BBQ sauce
3
125 ml (½ cup)

Smoked paprika
4
15 ml (1 tbsp)

Molasses
5
15 ml (1 tbsp)

ALSO NEEDED:
➤ **Garlic**
minced
15 ml (1 tbsp)

OPTIONAL:
➤ **Ground ginger**
15 ml (1 tbsp)

BBQ Pork Tenderloin

Prep time: **15 minutes** • Cook time on low: **5 hours** • Serves: **4**

Preparation

Trim the pork tenderloin by removing the silver skin.

In a bowl, mix the brown sugar, BBQ sauce, smoked paprika, molasses, garlic, and ground ginger, if desired. Season with salt and pepper.

Place the pork tenderloin in a large freezer bag. Add the sauce and close the bag. Shake to ensure the tenderloin is fully coated with the sauce. Remove the air from the bag and seal it.

Place the bag flat in the freezer.

The night before your meal, let the bag thaw out in the refrigerator.

When ready to cook, transfer the content of the bag to the slow cooker. Cover and cook on low for 5 to 6 hours.

PER SERVING	
Calories	331
Protein	38 g
Fat	3 g
Carbohydrates	37 g
Fibre	1 g
Iron	3 mg
Calcium	49 mg
Sodium	470 mg

Side Dish Idea

Pear and radish coleslaw

In a salad bowl, mix 60 ml (¼ cup) mayonnaise with 15 ml (1 tbsp) whole-grain mustard, 60 ml (¼ cup) orange juice, 45 ml (3 tbsp) chopped parsley, 30 ml (2 tbsp) honey and 30 ml (2 tbsp) chopped mint. Season with salt and pepper. Add half a green cabbage, finely chopped, 2 pears and 8 radishes, thinly sliced. Stir.

Diced tomatoes ❶
drained
1 can (540 ml)

Steak spice ❷
15 ml (1 tbsp)

Demi-glace sauce or beef gravy ❸
125 ml (½ cup)

Beef ❹
cubes for stew
720 g (about 1 ⅔ lb)

Bell peppers ❺
1 green and 1 red
cut into cubes

ALSO NEEDED:
➤ **1 onion**
chopped

➤ **Cornstarch**
15 ml (1 tbsp)

OPTIONAL:
➤ **Worcestershire sauce**
30 ml (2 tbsp)

Bell Pepper Beef

Prep time: **15 minutes** • Cook time on low: **6 hours** • Serves: **4**

Preparation

Place the diced tomatoes, steak spice, demi-glace sauce, onion, and Worcestershire sauce, if desired, in a large freezer bag. Close the bag and shake to mix.

Add the beef cubes to the bag and shake until the meat is fully coated with the sauce. Remove the air from the bag and seal it.

Place the bell peppers in another large freezer bag. Remove the air from the bag and seal it.

Place the bags flat in the freezer.

The night before your meal, let the bags thaw out in the refrigerator.

When ready to cook, transfer the beef preparation to the slow cooker. Cover and cook on low for 5 hours and 30 minutes to 6 hours and 30 minutes.

Drain the thawed bell peppers and add them to the slow cooker. Dissolve the cornstarch in a little cold water. Add to the slow cooker and stir.

Cover and continue cooking on low for 30 minutes.

Learn More

Demi-glace sauce

Demi-glace sauce is made with the reduction of a brown stock (veal or beef) that has simmered for close to 15 hours. It serves as a base for a number of sauces, giving them volume and a lot of flavour. Since it takes a fairly long time to prepare, you can take a shortcut by using store-bought demi-glace, like in this recipe. At the supermarket, you can find it frozen or refrigerated at the butcher counter or in pouches in the sauce aisle.

PER SERVING	
Calories	385
Protein	42 g
Fat	14 g
Carbohydrates	20 g
Fibre	2 g
Iron	6 mg
Calcium	89 mg
Sodium	720 mg

Chicken and Broccoli Casserole

Prep time: **15 minutes** • Cook time on low: **3 hours and 30 minutes** • Serves: **4**

**Condensed cream
of chicken soup**
1 can (284 ml)

❶

Chicken
4 skinless breasts
sliced

❷

2 carrots
diced

❸

Celery
2 stalks
diced

❹

Broccoli
1 stalk
cut into small florets

❺

Preparation

In a bowl, mix the cream of chicken soup with the chicken stock, shallots, and whole-grain mustard, if desired.

Place the chicken, carrots and celery in a large freezer bag. Pour the sauce into the bag and close it. Shake the bag until the ingredients are mixed well. Remove the air from the bag and seal it.

Place the broccoli in another large freezer bag. Remove the air from the bag and seal it.

Place the bags flat in the freezer.

The night before your meal, let the bags thaw out in the refrigerator.

When ready to cook, transfer the chicken preparation to the slow cooker. Cover and cook on low for 3 to 4 hours.

Drain the thawed broccoli and add it to the slow cooker. Cover and continue cooking on low for 30 minutes.

PER SERVING	
Calories	307
Protein	37 g
Fat	11 g
Carbohydrates	13 g
Fibre	2 g
Iron	1 mg
Calcium	50 mg
Sodium	957 mg

5•15 Tip

Thaw safely!

When you're using frozen chicken breasts in a recipe, you should avoid thawing them out at room temperature to prevent the growth of bacteria. If you forgot to put your chicken in the refrigerator the night before, you can thaw it out in the microwave (at 5 minutes per pound on the defrost setting) or in a bowl of cold water (fully submerge the chicken, in its packaging, and change the water every 30 minutes).

ALSO NEEDED:
➤ **Chicken stock**
125 ml (½ cup)

➤ **Shallots**
chopped
125 ml (½ cup)

OPTIONAL:
➤ **Whole-grain
mustard**
30 ml (2 tbsp)

Curry powder ❶
30 ml (2 tbsp)

Ground cumin ❷
5 ml (1 tsp)

Ginger ❸
grated
5 ml (1 tsp)

Cod ❹
560 g (about 1 ¼ lb)
cut into cubes

20 cherry tomatoes ❺

Cod Curry

Prep time: **15 minutes** • Cook time on low: **4 hours** • Serves: **4**

Preparation

In a bowl, mix the curry powder, cumin, ginger and vegetable stock. Season with salt and pepper.

In a large freezer bag, place the cod and cherry tomatoes. Pour the seasoned vegetable stock into the bag, and close it. Shake the bag until the ingredients are mixed well. Remove the air from the bag and seal it.

Place the bag flat in the freezer.

The night before your meal, let the bag thaw out in the refrigerator.

When ready to cook, transfer the content of the bag to the slow cooker. Cover and cook on low for 4 hours. Once it has finished cooking, adjust seasoning as needed.

Garnish with cilantro before serving, if desired.

PER SERVING	
Calories	150
Protein	27 g
Fat	2 g
Carbohydrates	7 g
Fibre	3 g
Iron	2 mg
Calcium	51 mg
Sodium	137 mg

Side Dish Idea

Lemon rice

Cook 125 ml (½ cup) basmati rice according to the package directions. Heat 15 ml (1 tbsp) olive oil in a frying pan over medium heat. Add half of a chopped onion and cook for 1 to 2 minutes. Add the cooked rice, 30 ml (2 tbsp) chopped parsley and 15 ml (1 tbsp) lemon zest. Season with salt and pepper.

ALSO NEEDED:
➤ **Vegetable stock**
low sodium
375 ml (1 ½ cups)

OPTIONAL:
➤ **Cilantro**
to taste

Recipe by Ève Godin, nutritionist

Veal ❶
stewing cubes
750 g (about 1 ⅔ lb)

1 red bell pepper ❷
diced

Celery ❸
2 stalks
diced

2 carrots ❹
diced

Red port wine ❺
375 ml (1 ½ cups)

ALSO NEEDED:
➤ **½ onion**
diced

Port Veal Stew

Prep time: **15 minutes** • Cook time on low: **8 hours** • Serves: **4**

Preparation

Place the veal, bell pepper, celery, carrot, port and onion in a large freezer bag. Shake until all the ingredients are fully coated with the port. Remove the air from the bag and seal it.

Place the bag flat in the freezer.

The night before your meal, let the bag thaw out in the refrigerator.

When ready to cook, transfer the content of the bag to the slow cooker. Cover and cook on low for 8 hours.

PER SERVING	
Calories	430
Protein	39 g
Fat	8 g
Carbohydrates	21 g
Fibre	2 g
Iron	2 mg
Calcium	60 mg
Sodium	199 mg

Side Dish Idea

Herbs and pine nuts tagliatelle

Cook 350 g (about ¾ lb) tagliatelle pasta *al dente* in a pot of boiling, salted water. Drain. In the same pot, heat 30 ml (2 tbsp) olive oil over medium heat. Cook 60 ml (¼ cup) pine nuts for 1 minute. Add the pasta, 30 ml (2 tbsp) chopped chives, 30 ml (2 tbsp) chopped parsley and 10 ml (2 tsp) chopped thyme. Season with salt and pepper, and stir well.

Pork ❶
tenderloins
755 g (1 ⅔ lb)

Shallots ❷
chopped
80 ml (⅓ cup)

Honey ❸
60 ml (¼ cup)

Whole-grain mustard ❹
45 ml (3 tbsp)

Worcestershire sauce ❺
30 ml (2 tbsp)

ALSO NEEDED:
➤ **Chicken stock**
125 ml (½ cup)
➤ **Cornstarch**
15 ml (1 tbsp)

OPTIONAL:
➤ **Thyme**
chopped
15 ml (1 tbsp)

Honey Mustard Pork

Prep time: **15 minutes** • Cook time on low: **5 hours** • Cook time on high: **15 minutes**
Serves: **4**

Preparation

Trim the pork tenderloins by removing the silver skin.

In a bowl, mix the shallots, honey, mustard, Worcestershire sauce and chicken stock. Season with salt and pepper.

Place the pork and thyme, if desired, in a large freezer bag. Pour the sauce into the bag and close it. Shake the bag until the ingredients are mixed well. Remove the air from the bag and seal it.

Place the bag flat in the freezer.

The night before your meal, let the bag thaw out in the refrigerator.

When ready to cook, transfer the content of the bag to the slow cooker. Cover and cook on low for 5 to 6 hours.

Remove the pork tenderloins from the slow cooker and place them on a plate. Cover them loosely with aluminum foil.

Dilute the cornstarch in a little cold water. Add it to the sauce in the slow cooker, whisking. Cover and continue cooking on high for 15 minutes. Serve the sauce with the pork tenderloins.

PER SERVING	
Calories	317
Protein	44 g
Fat	4 g
Carbohydrates	24 g
Fibre	0 g
Iron	3 mg
Calcium	29 mg
Sodium	602 mg

Side Dish Idea

Herb potatoes

In a pot of cold, salted water, place 450 g (1 lb) creamer potatoes. Bring to a boil and cook for 15 to 18 minutes, until the potatoes are cooked but still crunchy. Drain and cut the potatoes in half. Melt 15 ml (1 tbsp) butter in a large frying pan over medium heat. Roast the potatoes for 4 to 5 minutes. Transfer the potatoes to a large bowl. Add 15 ml (1 tbsp) olive oil, 15 ml (1 tbsp) lemon juice, 30 ml (2 tbsp) chopped parsley and 5 ml (1 tsp) chopped thyme. Season with salt and pepper.

Root beer
125 ml (½ cup) ①

Ketchup
80 ml (⅓ cup) ②

Molasses
20 ml (4 tsp) ③

Chicken
skinless breasts
675 g (about 1 ½ lb) ④

4 ciabatta buns ⑤

OPTIONAL:
➤ **Lettuce**
4 leaves

BBQ Pulled Chicken

Prep time: **15 minutes** • Cook time on low: **4 hours** • Cook time on high: **10 minutes** • Serves: **4**

Preparation

In a bowl, mix the root beer, ketchup and molasses. Season with salt and pepper.

Place the chicken breasts in a large freezer bag. Add the sauce and close the bag. Shake gently until the chicken is fully coated with the sauce. Remove the air from the bag and seal it.

Place the bag flat in the freezer.

The night before your meal, let the bag thaw out in the refrigerator.

When ready to cook, transfer the content of the bag to the slow cooker. Cover and cook on low for 4 to 5 hours.

Remove the chicken from the slow cooker and let it cool. Use two forks to shred the chicken.

Put the shredded chicken back into the slow cooker and stir. Cover and cook on high for 10 minutes.

Top the ciabatta buns with pulled chicken and garnish with lettuce, if desired.

PER SERVING	
Calories	423
Protein	44 g
Fat	5 g
Carbohydrates	48 g
Fibre	2 g
Iron	2 mg
Calcium	47 mg
Sodium	627 mg

Chef's Secret

For delicious slow-cooked meals every time

It's important to trim the fat from meat and poultry before slow-cooking it. Otherwise, that fat will melt and float up to the surface. For poultry, we recommend removing the skin too, which can get wrinkly in the slow cooker, or browning it first. Last but not least, searing meat before cooking it unlocks a whole lot of flavour and gives it an irresistible colour!

Root beer photo: Shutterstock

Beef 1
1 blade roast
900 g (2 lb)

Onion soup mix 2
1 pouch (42 g)

Creamer potatoes 3
cut in half
450 g (1 lb)

Green beans 4
150 g (⅓ lb)

Baby carrots 5
250 ml (1 cup)

Pot Roast with Vegetables

Prep time: **15 minutes** • Cook time on low: **8 hours** • Serves: **4**

Preparation

Place the blade roast in a large bowl. Sprinkle the onion soup mix over the roast and turn it to ensure the meat is fully coated.

Place the blade roast in a large freezer bag.

Add the potatoes, green beans and baby carrots to the bag. Season with salt and pepper. Remove the air from the bag and seal it.

Place the bag flat in the freezer.

The night before your meal, let the bag thaw out in the refrigerator.

When ready to cook, transfer the content the bag to the slow cooker. Add 250 ml (1 cup) water. Cover and cook on low for 8 to 9 hours.

PER SERVING	
Calories	473
Protein	50 g
Fat	15 g
Carbohydrates	32 g
Fibre	4 g
Iron	6 mg
Calcium	77 mg
Sodium	1,036 mg

5•15 Tip

The best cut of beef for the slow cooker

Beef is an excellent source of protein, potassium, zinc and certain B-complex vitamins, as well as iron and phosphorus. However, it's also a significant source of saturated fat and cholesterol. Tougher cuts that will tenderize as they cook are the best choice for the slow cooker, and they're more affordable too—blade, neck, shank and chuck roasts are all perfect for slow cooking at low heat!

Spicy chorizo ❶
150 g (⅓ lb)
cut into thick slices

Chickpeas ❷
rinsed and drained
1 can (540 ml)

Diced tomatoes ❸
1 can (796 ml)

4 bay leaves ❹

Paprika ❺
7.5 ml (½ tbsp)

ALSO NEEDED:
➤ **1 large onion**
chopped

OPTIONAL:
➤ **Garlic**
4 cloves
peeled and minced

Chickpea and Chorizo Stew

Prep time: **15 minutes** • Cook time on low: **5 hours** • Serves: **6**

Preparation

Place the chorizo, chickpeas and diced tomatoes in a large freezer bag. Shake to mix.

Add the bay leaves, paprika, onion, and garlic, if desired. Close the bag and shake to mix. Remove the air from the bag and seal it.

Place the bag flat in the freezer.

The night before your meal, let the bag thaw out in the refrigerator.

When ready to cook, transfer the content of the bag to the slow cooker. Cover and cook on low for 5 to 6 hours.

PER SERVING	
Calories	222
Protein	14 g
Fat	8 g
Carbohydrates	27 g
Fibre	4 g
Iron	4 mg
Calcium	92 mg
Sodium	657 mg

Learn More

Paprika

Paprika usually comes from Hungary or Spain. This deep red spice is made from a blend of ground peppers and adds both flavour and colour to dishes. There are many varieties of paprika, but the most common are sweet and smoked.

Apple and Sweet Potato Pork Chops

Prep time: **15 minutes** • Cook time on low: **6 hours** • Serves: **4**

Balsamic vinegar ❶
60 ml (¼ cup)

Brown sugar ❷
80 ml (⅓ cup)

3 sweet potatoes ❸
peeled and cut into
large cubes

3 Royal Gala apples ❹
peeled and cut
into wedges

Pork ❺
4 chops
2.5 cm (1 in) thick

ALSO NEEDED:
➤ **½ red onion**
cut into wedges

Preparation

In a large bowl, mix the vinegar, brown sugar, sweet potatoes, apples, pork chops and red onion. Season with salt and pepper.

Transfer the ingredients to a large freezer bag. Remove the air from the bag and seal it.

Place the bag flat in the freezer.

The night before your meal, let the bag thaw out in the refrigerator.

When ready to cook, transfer the content of the bag to the slow cooker. Cover and cook on low for 6 to 7 hours.

PER SERVING	
Calories	344
Protein	25 g
Fat	5 g
Carbohydrates	50 g
Fibre	5 g
Iron	2 mg
Calcium	70 mg
Sodium	120 mg

Healthy Choice

Sweet potato

This recipe is an excellent way to add the delicious sweet potato to the menu! Its nutritious orange flesh is chock-full of vitamins and minerals. It's also a great source of vitamin A, an antioxidant compound that plays an important role in keeping your eyes and skin healthy. Sweet potatoes are satisfying and high in fibre, and they're sweeter than regular potatoes. So why not mix it up? Swap in a sweet potato instead of a regular potato in your next recipe!

3 bell pepper halves ❶
various colours

Chicken ❷
4 skinless breasts
cut in half
lengthwise

Broccoli ❸
1 stalk
cut into small florets

Maple syrup ❹
125 ml (½ cup)

Apple cider vinegar ❺
30 ml (2 tbsp)

ALSO NEEDED:
➤ **2 small red onions**
➤ **Garlic**
minced
15 ml (1 tbsp)

OPTIONAL:
➤ **Fresh herbs of your choice**
chopped
60 ml (¼ cup)

Maple-glazed Chicken
Prep time: **15 minutes** • Cook time: **30 minutes** • Serves: **4**

Preparation

Slice the bell peppers and cut the red onions into wedges.

Place the chicken breasts, broccoli, peppers, red onions, maple syrup, apple cider vinegar, garlic, and herbs, if desired, in a large freezer bag. Season with salt and pepper. Close the bag and shake until the ingredients are fully coated with the marinade. Remove the air from the bag and seal it.

Place the bag flat in the freezer.

The night before your meal, let the bag thaw out in the refrigerator.

When ready to cook, preheat the oven to 205°C (400°F).

Transfer the ingredients to a baking dish. Bake for 30 to 35 minutes, until the chicken is no longer pink in the centre.

PER SERVING	
Calories	373
Protein	43 g
Fat	3 g
Carbohydrates	43 g
Fibre	2 g
Iron	3 mg
Calcium	125 mg
Sodium	128 mg

Learn More

Maple syrup

Did you know that maple syrup contains 54 antioxidants, including a high concentration of polyphenols? To date, 63 types of polyphenols have been identified in this syrup, including "Quebecol," named in honour of Quebec, of course! These polyphenols help fight against free radicals that can cause cardiovascular and inflammatory diseases. The antioxidants in maple syrup are also thought to play a role in preventing type 2 diabetes.

Fajita seasoning ❶
1 pouch (35 g)

Lime juice ❷
30 ml (2 tbsp)

3 bell pepper halves ❸
various colours
sliced

2 small red onions ❹
sliced

Salmon ❺
fillets
675 g (about 1 ½ lb)
skin removed
and cut into cubes

ALSO NEEDED:
➤ **Olive oil**
30 ml (2 tbsp)

➤ **Cilantro**
45 ml (3 tbsp)

OPTIONAL:
➤ **8 small tortillas**

Fajita-style Salmon

Prep time: **15 minutes** • Cook time: **20 minutes** • Serves: 4

Preparation

In a bowl, mix the olive oil with the fajita seasoning, lime juice and cilantro.

Transfer the marinade into a large freezer bag. Add the peppers, red onion and salmon cubes. Close the bag and shake it to ensure the ingredients are fully coated with the marinade. Remove the air from the bag and seal it.

Place the bag flat in the freezer.

The night before your meal, let the bag thaw out in the refrigerator.

When ready to cook, preheat the oven to 205°C (400°F).

Spread the prepared ingredients on a baking sheet. Bake for 20 to 25 minutes.

Serve on tortillas, if desired.

PER SERVING	
Calories	668
Protein	41 g
Fat	34 g
Carbohydrates	46 g
Fibre	3 g
Iron	2 mg
Calcium	38 mg
Sodium	1,276 mg

Side Dish Idea

Spicy sour cream

Mix 80 ml (⅓ cup) sour cream with 60 ml (¼ cup) mayonnaise, 30 ml (2 tbsp) ketchup and 2 to 3 drops Tabasco sauce. Season with salt.

Soy sauce ①
45 ml (3 tbsp)

Lemon juice ②
30 ml (2 tbsp)

Balsamic vinegar ③
15 ml (1 tbsp)

Cumin seeds ④
5 ml (1 tsp)

Pork ⑤
1 tenderloin
750 g (1 ⅔ lb)
silver skin removed

ALSO NEEDED:
➤ **Olive oil**
60 ml (¼ cup)

Balsamic Pork Tenderloin

Prep time: **15 minutes** • Cook time: **25 minutes** • Serves: **4**

Preparation

Place the soy sauce, lemon juice, balsamic vinegar, cumin seeds and olive oil in a large freezer bag. Close the bag and shake to mix. Add the pork tenderloin, then close the bag and shake until the pork is fully coated with the marinade. Remove the air from the bag and seal it.

Place the bag flat in the freezer.

The night before your meal, let the bag thaw out in the refrigerator.

When ready to cook, preheat the oven to 205°C (400°F).

Spread the preparation on a baking sheet. Bake for 25 to 30 minutes.

Transfer the pork tenderloin to a plate and cover it loosely with aluminum foil. Let it rest for a few minutes before slicing it.

PER SERVING	
Calories	234
Protein	42 g
Fat	6 g
Carbohydrates	1 g
Fibre	0 g
Iron	2 mg
Calcium	13 mg
Sodium	258 mg

Side Dish Idea

Lime and poppy seed coleslaw

In a salad bowl, mix 60 ml (¼ cup) sesame oil (not toasted) with 30 ml (2 tbsp) lime juice, 30 ml (2 tbsp) honey, 15 ml (1 tbsp) lime zest and 15 ml (1 tbsp) poppy seeds. Season with salt and pepper. Add 1 bag of coleslaw vegetable mix (454 g) and 60 ml (¼ cup) chopped parsley. Stir.

Chicken stock ❶
250 ml (1 cup)

Tomato pesto or sun-dried tomato pesto ❷
80 ml (⅓ cup)

Cooking cream (15%) ❸
125 ml (½ cup)

Basil ❹
chopped
60 ml (¼ cup)

Chicken ❺
4 skinless breasts

ALSO NEEDED:
➤ **1 onion**
chopped
➤ **Garlic**
minced
15 ml (1 tbsp)

OPTIONAL:
➤ **Capers**
15 ml (1 tbsp)

Creamy Tomato Chicken

Prep time: **15 minutes** • Cook time: **20 minutes** • Serves: **4**

Preparation

In a bowl, whisk the chicken stock, pesto, cream, basil, onion, garlic, and capers, if desired. Season with salt and pepper. Pour the sauce into a large freezer bag. Add the chicken breasts. Close the bag and shake until the chicken is fully coated with the sauce. Remove the air from the bag and seal it.

Place the bag flat in the freezer.

The night before your meal, let the bag thaw out in the refrigerator.

When ready to cook, preheat the oven to 180°C (350°F).

Transfer the chicken and sauce to a 20 cm (8 in) square baking dish. Bake for 20 to 25 minutes, until the chicken is no longer pink in the centre.

PER SERVING	
Calories	390
Protein	42 g
Fat	20 g
Carbohydrates	8 g
Fibre	2 g
Iron	1 mg
Calcium	59 mg
Sodium	534 mg

Homemade Version

Sun-dried tomato pesto

Use a blender to puree 250 ml (1 cup) minced oil-packed sun-dried tomatoes, 2 garlic cloves, 5 ml (1 tsp) chopped thyme and 125 ml (½ cup) toasted pine nuts. Add 60 ml (¼ cup) olive oil and blend until smooth and consistent. Add 125 ml (½ cup) grated parmesan and blend for a few more seconds. Season with salt and pepper. This recipe makes 500 ml (2 cups) of pesto.

Roast gravy mix **1**
2 pouches
(34 g each)

Red wine **2**
250 ml (1 cup)

Baby carrots **3**
500 ml (2 cups)

Whole white potatoes **4**
drained
1 can (540 ml)

Beef **5**
sirloin steak
650 g (about 1 ½ lb)
cut into strips

ALSO NEEDED:
➤ **Beef stock**
no salt added
310 ml (1 ¼ cups)

➤ **Thyme**
1 sprig
chopped

Red Wine Braised Beef

Prep time: **15 minutes** • Cook time: **30 minutes** • Serves: **6**

Preparation

In a bowl, mix the contents of the roast gravy mix pouches with red wine, beef stock and thyme. Season with pepper.

Transfer the sauce to a large freezer bag. Add the baby carrots, potatoes and beef. Close the bag and shake until the ingredients are fully coated with the sauce. Remove the air from the bag and seal it.

Place the bag flat in the freezer.

The night before your meal, let the bag thaw out in the refrigerator.

When ready to cook, preheat the oven to 205°C (400°F).

Transfer the ingredients to a 33 cm x 23 cm (13 in x 9 in) baking dish. Cover with aluminum foil and bake for 30 to 35 minutes.

PER SERVING	
Calories	259
Protein	27 g
Fat	6 g
Carbohydrates	16 g
Fibre	1 g
Iron	3 mg
Calcium	40 mg
Sodium	904 mg

Side Dish Idea

Sautéed snow peas with ginger

Cook 500 ml (2 cups) snow peas in a pot of boiling, salted water for 4 to 5 minutes. Drain. Heat 15 ml (1 tbsp) canola oil in a large frying pan over medium heat. Add 15 ml (1 tbsp) minced ginger and the snow peas and cook for 1 to 2 minutes, stirring. Add 15 ml (1 tbsp) toasted sesame seeds, 15 ml (1 tbsp) soy sauce and 15 ml (1 tbsp) sesame oil. Stir.

Orange juice ❶
125 ml (½ cup)

Vegetable stock ❷
125 ml (½ cup)

Honey ❸
30 ml (2 tbsp)

Ginger ❹
minced
15 ml (1 tbsp)

Firm tofu ❺
1 block (454 g)

ALSO NEEDED:
➤ **Garlic**
minced
15 ml (1 tbsp)
➤ **2 green onions**
chopped

OPTIONAL:
➤ **Thyme**
chopped
15 ml (1 tbsp)

One Pan Honey Ginger Tofu

Prep time: **15 minutes** • Cook time: **10 minutes** • Serves: **4**

Preparation

In a bowl, mix the orange juice, vegetable stock, honey, ginger, garlic, green onions, and thyme, if desired.

Cut the block of tofu into 8 slices widthwise. Place the slices in a large freezer bag and cover with the marinade. Close the bag and shake until the tofu is fully coated with the marinade. Remove the air from the bag and seal it.

Place the bag flat in the freezer.

The night before your meal, let the bag thaw out in the refrigerator.

When ready to cook, preheat the oven to 205°C (400°F).

Drain the tofu, keeping the marinade.

Line a baking sheet with parchment paper and place the tofu slices on it. Cover with the reserved marinade.

Bake for 10 to 12 minutes.

PER SERVING	
Calories	137
Protein	17 g
Fat	8 g
Carbohydrates	16 g
Fibre	0 g
Iron	2 mg
Calcium	189 mg
Sodium	112 mg

Side Dish Idea

Green and yellow beans with orange

Line a baking sheet with parchment paper and spread 200 g (about ½ lb) green and yellow beans over it. Slice 1 orange in half circles, then spread them over the beans. Bake for 10 to 12 minutes at 205°C (400°F). Remove them from the oven and sprinkle with 10 ml (2 tsp) sesame seeds.

Chicken ❶
4 skinless legs
cut in half

1 green bell pepper ❷
cut in cubes

3 tomatoes ❸
diced

Smoked paprika ❹
15 ml (1 tbsp)

Cooking cream (15%) ❺
125 ml (½ cup)

ALSO NEEDED:
➤ **1 onion**
diced
➤ **Chicken stock**
250 ml (1 cup)

Smoked Paprika Chicken Legs

Prep time: **15 minutes** • Cook time: **46 minutes** • Serves: **4**

Preparation

In a large freezer bag, place the chicken pieces, bell pepper, tomatoes, paprika, diced onion and chicken stock. Close the bag and shake to mix. Remove the air from the bag and seal it.

Place the bag flat in the freezer.

The night before your meal, let the bag thaw out in the refrigerator.

When ready to cook, preheat the oven to 190°C (375°F).

Place the prepared content of the bag in a baking dish. Bake for 40 to 45 minutes, until the meat is no longer pink in the centre and the flesh comes away from the bone easily.

Add the cream to the baking dish and bake for another 6 to 7 minutes.

Divide the chicken pieces and vegetables onto plates and top with the cream sauce.

PER SERVING	
Calories	321
Protein	29 g
Fat	18 g
Carbohydrates	12 g
Fibre	3 g
Iron	2 mg
Calcium	68 mg
Sodium	365 mg

Side Dish Idea

Egg noodles with chives and butter

Cook 250 g (about ½ lb) egg noodles *al dente* in a pot of boiling, salted water. Drain. In the same pot, heat 30 ml (2 tbsp) butter until it starts to brown. Remove from heat. Add 30 ml (2 tbsp) chopped chives and noodles. Season with pepper, and stir.

10 eggs ①

Cooking cream (15%) ②
80 ml (⅓ cup)

Sharp cheddar ③
shredded
250 ml (1 cup)

Ham ④
diced
375 ml (1 ½ cups)

**Fresh herbs
of your choice** ⑤
chopped
80 ml (⅓ cup)

ALSO NEEDED:
➤ **Garlic**
minced
15 ml (1 tbsp)
➤ **Olive oil**
30 ml (2 tbsp)

Ham and Cheddar Frittata

Prep time: **15 minutes** • Cook time: **30 minutes** • Serves: 4

Preparation

In a large bowl, whisk the eggs, cream, cheddar, ham, herbs, garlic and oil. Season with salt and pepper. Transfer the preparation to a large freezer bag. Remove the air from the bag and seal it.

Place the bag flat in the freezer.

The night before your meal, let the bag thaw out in the refrigerator.

When ready to cook, preheat the oven to 180°C (350°F).

Grease a 20 cm (8 in) square baking dish or a few ramekins, and pour in the prepared ingredients. Bake for 30 to 35 minutes, until the frittata is set.

PER SERVING	
Calories	443
Protein	29 g
Fat	34 g
Carbohydrates	6 g
Fibre	1 g
Iron	3 mg
Calcium	215 mg
Sodium	982 mg

Good To Know

The difference between an omelette and a frittata

It's easy to confuse omelettes and frittatas, since they're both egg dishes that can be dressed up many different ways. So what's the difference? It's the way they're prepared! Frittata is an Italian dish that's baked in the oven. It's thicker and looks like a Spanish tortilla. Omelettes, on the other hand, are cooked in a frying pan over medium heat and then folded in half to cover the toppings placed on the eggs as they cook.

Beef ❶
600 g (about 1 ⅓ lb)
cut into cubes

1 green zucchini ❷
cut into cubes

1 red bell pepper ❸
cut into cubes

12 mushrooms ❹

BBQ sauce ❺
310 ml (1 ¼ cups)

ALSO NEEDED:
➤ **1 onion**
cut into cubes

BBQ Beef and Vegetable Skewers

Prep time: **15 minutes** • Soaking (optional): **30 minutes** • Cook time: **12 minutes** • Serves: 4

Preparation

In a large freezer bag, place the beef cubes, zucchini, bell pepper, mushrooms and onion. Remove the air from the bag and seal it.

Place the bag flat in the freezer.

The night before your meal, let the bag thaw out in the refrigerator.

If you're using bamboo skewers, soak them in water for about 30 minutes before cooking.

When ready to cook, preheat the oven to 220°C (425°F).

Thread the beef cubes onto the skewers, alternating with the vegetable cubes and the mushrooms.

Place the skewers on a baking sheet lined with parchment paper.

Bake for 12 to 15 minutes, turning the skewers halfway through cooking time and brushing them with half of the BBQ sauce. Serve with the rest of the sauce.

PER SERVING	
Calories	410
Protein	35 g
Fat	12 g
Carbohydrates	38 g
Fibre	2 g
Iron	4 mg
Calcium	37 mg
Sodium	1,021 mg

Side Dish Idea

Roasted asparagus and almonds

Mix 12 stalks of asparagus with 15 ml (1 tbsp) softened butter in a large bowl. Season with salt and pepper. Spread the asparagus on a baking sheet lined with parchment paper. Roast in the oven for 4 to 5 minutes at 205°C (400°F). Sprinkle with 125 ml (½ cup) sliced almonds and continue roasting for another 4 to 5 minutes.

Dill ①
chopped
30 ml (2 tbsp)

Lemon ②
15 ml (1 tbsp) juice +
15 ml (1 tbsp) zest

20 cherry tomatoes ③
various colours
cut in half

Pancetta or bacon ④
6 slices
cut into pieces

**Medium shrimp
(31-40 count)** ⑤
raw and peeled
1 bag (340 g)

ALSO NEEDED:
➤ **Olive oil**
60 ml (¼ cup)

➤ **Garlic**
minced
5 ml (1 tsp)

OPTIONAL:
➤ **Paprika**
10 ml (2 tsp)

➤ **Chives**
chopped
45 ml (3 tbsp)

One Pan Shrimp and Pancetta

Prep time: **15 minutes** • Cook time: **12 minutes** • Serves: **4**

Preparation

In a bowl, whisk the olive oil, dill, lemon juice, lemon zest, garlic, and paprika, if desired.

Transfer the marinade to a large freezer bag. Add the cherry tomatoes, pancetta, shrimp, and chives, if desired. Season with salt. Close the bag and shake until the ingredients are fully coated with the marinade. Remove the air from the bag and seal it.

Place the bag flat in the freezer.

The night before your meal, let the bag thaw out in the refrigerator.

When ready to cook, preheat the oven to 205°C (400°F).

Spread the prepared ingredients on a baking sheet lined with parchment paper. Bake for 12 to 15 minutes.

PER SERVING	
Calories	230
Protein	15 g
Fat	17 g
Carbohydrates	5 g
Fibre	2 g
Iron	1 mg
Calcium	62 mg
Sodium	593 mg

Learn More

Pancetta

This delicious Italian charcuterie is made from pork belly that has been cured and dried for three months, then rolled to make a large sausage. It looks quite similar to bacon (which can easily replace pancetta in a recipe), is usually cut in thin slices and can be eaten cold or cooked. You may know pancetta as the star ingredient of a carbonara sauce, but it can also be added to soups, pizzas and other sauces, with delightful results.

Oven Baked

Apple jelly
125 ml (½ cup) ❶

Ketchup
80 ml (⅓ cup) ❷

Worcestershire sauce
30 ml (2 tbsp) ❸

Apple cider vinegar
30 ml (2 tbsp) ❹

Chicken
32 wings ❺

ALSO NEEDED:
➤ **Onion powder**
30 ml (2 tbsp)

➤ **Garlic**
minced
15 ml (1 tbsp)

OPTIONAL:
➤ **Paprika**
5 ml (1 tsp)

Apple Jelly Chicken Wings

Prep time: **15 minutes** • Cook time: **20 minutes** • Serves: **8**

Preparation

Place the apple jelly, ketchup, Worcestershire sauce, vinegar, onion powder, garlic, a little olive oil, and paprika, if desired, in a large freezer bag. Close the bag and shake to mix. Add the chicken wings and close the bag. Shake the bag again until the wings are fully coated in the sauce. Remove the air from the bag and seal it.

Place the bag flat in the freezer.

The night before your meal, let the bag thaw out in the refrigerator.

When ready to eat, preheat the oven to 205°C (400°F).

Spread the chicken wings on a baking sheet lined with parchment paper. Bake for 20 to 25 minutes.

PER SERVING	
Calories	465
Protein	35 g
Fat	28 g
Carbohydrates	19 g
Fibre	1 g
Iron	1 mg
Calcium	38 mg
Sodium	303 mg

Side Dish Idea

Light fries with paprika

Cut 4 to 5 potatoes into sticks and place them in a bowl. Mix with 30 ml (2 tbsp) canola oil, 5 ml (1 tsp) paprika and 10 ml (2 tsp) chopped thyme. Season with salt. Spread the potatoes in a single layer on a baking sheet lined with parchment paper. Bake for 20 to 25 minutes at 205°C (400°F).

Edamame
375 ml (1 ½ cup) ❶

Saumon ❷
fillets
675 g (1 ½ lb)
skin removed
and cut into cubes

Honey mustard ❸
vinaigrette
180 ml (¾ cup)

1 yellow bell pepper ❹
diced

18 cherry tomatoes ❺

One Pan Salmon, Edamame and Vegetables

Prep time: **15 minutes** • Cook time: **12 minutes** • Serves: **4**

Preparation

In a pot of boiling, salted water, cook the edamame for 3 minutes. Drain and let cool.

Place the salmon cubes and half of the vinaigrette in a large freezer bag. Season with salt and pepper.

Close the bag and shake until the salmon is fully coated with the vinaigrette. Remove the air from the bag and seal it.

Place the bell pepper, cherry tomatoes, red onion, and asparagus, if desired, in a second large freezer bag. Add the rest of the vinaigrette. Season with salt and pepper. Close the bag and shake until the ingredients are fully coated with the vinaigrette. Remove the air from the bag and seal it.

Place the edamame in a third freezer bag. Remove the air from the bag and seal it.

Place the bags flat in the freezer.

The night before your meal, let the bags thaw out in the refrigerator.

When ready to cook, preheat the oven to 205°C (400°F).

Spread the salmon cubes on a baking sheet lined with parchment paper. Bake for 3 minutes.

Add the vegetables from the second bag and bake for 10 to 12 minutes. About 3 minutes before the end of the cook time, add the edamame from the third bag to the sheet. Bake until the salmon flakes easily with a fork.

Serve with lemon wedges. Sprinkle with mint leaves, if desired.

PER SERVING	
Calories	765
Protein	51 g
Fat	49 g
Carbohydrates	34 g
Fibre	8 g
Iron	6 mg
Calcium	259 mg
Sodium	358 mg

Homemade Version

Honey mustard vinaigrette

In a bowl, mix 125 ml (½ cup) olive oil, 30 ml (2 tbsp) lemon juice, 30 ml (2 tbsp) chopped chives, 15 ml (1 tbsp) honey, 15 ml (1 tbsp) whole-grain mustard and 15 ml (1 tbsp) chopped thyme. Season with salt and pepper. Stir.

ALSO NEEDED:
➤ **1 small red onion**
cut into wedges
➤ **1 lemon**
cut into wedges

OPTIONAL:
➤ **12 asparagus**
cut into pieces
➤ **Mint**
12 small leaves

Oregano ❶
chopped
30 ml (2 tbsp)

Lemon juice ❷
15 ml (1 tbsp)

Garlic ❸
minced
15 ml (1 tbsp)

Pork ❹
1 tenderloin
450 g (1 lb)
cut in small cubes

4 Greek pitas ❺

ALSO NEEDED:
➤ **Olive oil**
30 ml (2 tbsp)
➤ **½ red onion**
diced

OPTIONAL:
➤ **Green leaf lettuce**
8 leaves
➤ **2 tomatoes**
sliced

Pork Gyros

Prep time: **15 minutes** • Soaking (optional): **30 minutes** • Cook time: **10 minutes** • Serves: **4**

Preparation

In a bowl, whisk the olive oil, oregano, lemon juice and garlic. Season with salt and pepper.

Transfer the marinade into a large freezer bag. Add the pork cubes. Close the bag and shake until the cubes are fully coated with the marinade. Remove the air from the bag and seal it.

Place the bag flat in the freezer.

The night before your meal, let the bag thaw out in the refrigerator.

If you're using bamboo skewers, soak them in cold water for about 30 minutes before cooking.

When ready to cook, preheat the oven to 180°C (350°F).

Drain the pork cubes and discard the marinade. Thread the pork cubes onto the skewers.

Place the skewers on a baking sheet lined with parchment paper. Bake for 10 to 12 minutes, turning the skewers halfway through cooking time.

Top the pitas with the pork skewers, red onion, and if desired, lettuce, tomato and tzatziki (see recipe below). Remove the skewers, and then wrap the pitas around the filling.

PER SERVING	
Calories	419
Protein	31 g
Fat	10 g
Carbohydrates	53 g
Fibre	3 g
Iron	4 mg
Calcium	84 mg
Sodium	451 mg

Side Dish Idea

Tzatziki

Peel, seed and grate half a cucumber into a bowl with 15 ml (1 tbsp) coarse salt. Transfer to a strainer and let drain for 30 minutes. Transfer the cucumber back to the bowl and add one clove minced garlic, 250 ml (1 cup) plain Greek yogourt and 15 ml (1 tbsp) olive oil. Season with salt, and stir.

3 bell peppers ①
various colours
sliced

Chicken stock ②
low sodium
125 ml (½ cup)

1 garlic clove ③
minced

Cod ④
4 fillets
150 g (⅓ lb) each

Harissa
or sambal oelek ⑤
30 ml (2 tbsp)

ALSO NEEDED:
➤ **Olive oil**
15 ml (1 tbsp)

OPTIONAL:
➤ **Kosher salt**
to taste
➤ **Lemon juice**
15 ml (1 tbsp)

Spicy Cod and Bell Peppers

Prep time: **5 minutes** • Cook time: **20 minutes** • Serves: 4

Preparation

In a large freezer bag, place the bell peppers, chicken stock, garlic and olive oil. Close the bag and shake to mix. Remove the air from the bag and seal it.

In another large freezer bag, place the cod fillets and harissa. Close the bag and shake to mix. Remove the air from the bag and seal it.

Place the bags flat in the freezer.

The night before your meal, let the bags thaw out in the refrigerator.

When ready to cook, preheat the oven to 205°C (400°F).

Spread the bell peppers on a baking sheet lined with parchment paper. Bake for 5 minutes.

Place the cod fillets on top of the peppers. Sprinkle with salt, if desired. Bake for 15 minutes, until the fish flakes easily with a fork.

When ready to serve, sprinkle with lemon juice, if desired.

Learn More

Harissa

Harissa is a very spicy sauce made from roasted hot peppers, seasonings and olive oil. It's a common ingredient in Maghrebi cuisine, where it adds spice and flavour to tajines and couscous. Use it with moderation, as it could overpower the taste of the other ingredients in the dish or cause an unpleasant surprise for your dinner guests!

PER SERVING	
Calories	171
Protein	16 g
Fat	4 g
Carbohydrates	8 g
Fibre	1 g
Iron	1 mg
Calcium	26 mg
Sodium	378 mg

Chicken and Broccoli Rice Casserole

Prep time: **15 minutes** • Cook time: **25 minutes** • Serves: 4

Condensed cream of mushroom
low sodium
2 cans (284 ml each)
1

Italian-style shredded 4 cheese blend
500 ml (2 cups)
2

Rice
cooked
1.25 litre (5 cups)
3

Broccoli
cut in small florets
500 ml (2 cups)
4

Chicken
cut into small pieces
500 ml (2 cups)
5

Preparation

In a large bowl, mix the cream of mushroom and shredded cheese. Add the cooked rice, broccoli, chicken and 250 ml (1 cup) water. Season with salt and pepper. Mix well.

Transfer the prepared ingredients to a large freezer bag. Remove the air from the bag and seal it.

Place the bag flat in the freezer.

The night before your meal, let the bag thaw out in the refrigerator.

When ready to cook, preheat the oven to 180°C (350°F).

Transfer the content of the bag to a 33 cm x 23 cm (13 in x 9 in) baking dish and level out the surface. Bake for 25 to 30 minutes, until the chicken is no longer pink in the centre.

PER SERVING	
Calories	692
Protein	42 g
Fat	20 g
Carbohydrates	84 g
Fibre	1 g
Iron	1 mg
Calcium	399 mg
Sodium	805 mg

5•15 Tip

Stock up on cooked rice, in the freezer!

Rice that's ready in 5 minutes, impossible, you say? To pull off this incredible feat, just look to your freezer. Cooked rice can be frozen for 6 to 8 months in an airtight container. So why not double your recipes and freeze the extra for those busy nights? You can then simply pull out a container from the freezer before you leave for work in the morning and let it thaw out in the refrigerator. When you get home, you'll just have to reheat the rice in the microwave, adding a little liquid if needed. If you're making rice with vegetables, add it to the pan in the last minutes of cooking.

Steak spice
15 ml (1 tbsp) ❶

Honey ❷
45 ml (3 tbsp)

8 mild Italian ❸
sausages

Baby carrots ❹
250 ml (1 cup)

3 Royal Gala apples ❺
peeled and
cut into wedges

ALSO NEEDED:
➤ **Olive oil**
30 ml (2 tbsp)

➤ **1 onion**
diced

One Pan Sausages and Apples

Prep time: **15 minutes** • Cook time: **30 minutes** • Serves: **4**

Preparation

In a bowl, mix the oil, steak spice and honey.

Transfer the preparation to a large freezer bag. Add the sausages, baby carrots, apple and onion. Season with salt and pepper. Close the bag and shake until the ingredients are fully coated. Remove the air from the bag and seal it.

Place the bag flat in the freezer.

The night before your meal, let the bag thaw out in the refrigerator.

When ready to cook, preheat the oven to 205°C (400°F).

Spread the ingredients on a baking sheet. Bake for 30 to 35 minutes.

PER SERVING	
Calories	584
Protein	21 g
Fat	37 g
Carbohydrates	45 g
Fibre	5 g
Iron	1 mg
Calcium	33 mg
Sodium	1,163 mg

Mix It Up

Choose different sausages

Change up the flavours in this recipe by using different kinds of sausages! Go for a mix of different meats (pork and veal, pork and beef, turkey) or a flavoured version (spicy, honey garlic, maple chipotle or cheddar and bacon). The options are many! Try it too with Polish sausages, bratwurst or even classic smoked sausages.

Lemon juice
1
60 ml (¼ cup)

Thyme
2
chopped
5 ml (1 tsp)

Ground cumin
3
5 ml (1 tsp)

1 shallot
4
diced

Beef
5
675 g (about 1 ½ lb)
cubes for skewers

ALSO NEEDED:
➤ **Olive oil**
15 ml (1 tbsp)
➤ **Garlic**
1 clove
minced

OPTIONAL:
➤ **Cayenne pepper**
1 pinch
➤ **4 to 8 pitas**

Beef Kebabs

Prep time: **15 minutes** • Soaking (optional): **30 minutes** • Cook time: **12 minutes** • Serves: **4**

Preparation

In a bowl, whisk the olive oil, lemon juice, thyme, cumin, shallot, garlic and cayenne pepper, if desired.

Transfer the marinade to a large freezer bag. Add the beef cubes. Close the bag and shake until the beef cubes are fully coated with the marinade. Remove the air from the bag and seal it.

Place the bag flat in the freezer.

The night before your meal, let the bag thaw out in the refrigerator.

If you're using bamboo skewers, soak them in water for about 30 minutes before cooking.

When ready to cook, preheat the oven to 220°C (425°F). Drain the beef cubes and discard the marinade.

Thread the beef cubes onto the skewers.

Place the skewers on a baking sheet lined with parchment paper. Bake for 12 to 15 minutes, turning the skewers halfway through cooking time.

Serve the kebabs with pitas, if desired.

PER SERVING	
Calories	473
Protein	42 g
Fat	18 g
Carbohydrates	32 g
Fibre	1 g
Iron	5 mg
Calcium	61 mg
Sodium	412 mg

Side Dish Idea

Spicy tomato sauce

In a pot, mix 250 ml (1 cup) tomato sauce with 80 ml (⅓ cup) water, 15 ml (1 tbsp) olive oil, 15 ml (1 tbsp) tomato paste and 1.25 ml (¼ tsp) cayenne pepper. Season with salt. Bring to a boil, and then simmer for 10 minutes on low heat.

Cream of asparagus (prepared)
250 ml (1 cup)

❶

1 orange bell pepper
diced

❷

Tarragon
chopped
30 ml (2 tbsp)

❸

Cajun seasoning
15 ml (1 tbsp)

❹

Chicken
4 skinless breasts

❺

Asparagus Chicken en Papillote

Prep time: **15 minutes** • Cook time: **20 minutes** • Serves: **4**

PER SERVING	
Calories	228
Protein	42 g
Fat	4 g
Carbohydrates	6 g
Fibre	1 g
Fer	1 mg
Calcium	20 mg
Sodium	284 mg

Preparation

In a bowl, mix the prepared cream of asparagus, bell pepper, tarragon and Cajun seasoning.

Transfer the sauce to a large freezer bag. Add the chicken breasts. Close the bag and shake until the chicken is fully coated with the sauce. Remove the air from the bag and seal it.

Place the bag flat in the freezer.

The night before your meal, let the bag thaw out in the refrigerator.

When ready to cook, preheat the oven to 205°C (400°F).

Place each chicken breast at the centre of a large sheet of aluminum foil. Pour the cream of asparagus sauce over each breast.

Fold the foil into closed packages, and place them on a baking sheet.

Bake for 20 to 25 minutes, until the chicken is no longer pink in the centre.

Side Dish Idea

Green and yellow beans with pine nuts

Cook 450 g (1 lb) green and yellow beans for 3 to 4 minutes in a pot of boiling, salted water. Drain. In a frying pan, melt 30 ml (2 tbsp) butter over medium heat. Add 1 chopped onion, 30 ml (2 tbsp) pine nuts and 5 ml (1 tsp) minced garlic and cook for 2 to 3 minutes. Add the beans and cook for 1 to 2 minutes. Season with salt and pepper, and stir.

Orange juice ①
250 ml (1 cup)

Shallots ②
chopped
60 ml (¼ cup)

Honey ③
45 ml (3 tbsp)

Rosemary ④
chopped
15 ml (1 tbsp)

Salmon ⑤
4 fillets
180 g (about ⅓ lb) each
2.5 cm (1 in) thick
skin removed

ALSO NEEDED:
➤ **Olive oil**
30 ml (2 tbsp)
➤ **Cornstarch**
15 ml (1 tbsp)

FACULTATIF :
➤ **Garlic**
minced
5 ml (1 tsp)

Orange Rosemary Glazed Salmon

Prep time: **10 minutes** • Cook time: **18 minutes** • Serves: **4**

Preparation

In a large freezer bag, place the orange juice, shallots, honey, rosemary, olive oil, cornstarch and garlic, if desired. Season with salt and pepper. Close the bag and shake to mix. Add the salmon fillets to the bag. Close the bag and shake until the fillets are fully coated with the marinade. Remove the air from the bag and seal it.

Place the bag flat in the freezer.

The night before your meal, let the bag thaw out in the refrigerator.

When ready to cook, preheat the oven to 205°C (400°F).

Place the salmon fillets and marinade in a baking dish. Bake for 18 to 20 minutes.

PER SERVING	
Calories	530
Protein	38 g
Fat	31 g
Carbohydrates	24 g
Fibre	0 g
Iron	1 mg
Calcium	31 mg
Sodium	109 mg

Side Dish Idea

Couscous with herbs

In a bowl, mix 250 ml (1 cup) couscous with 30 ml (2 tbsp) olive oil. Season with salt and pepper. Pour in 250 ml (1 cup) of very hot chicken stock. Cover and let the couscous steam for 5 minutes. Fluff the couscous with a fork. Add 30 ml (2 tbsp) chopped chives and 30 ml (2 tbsp) chopped parsley. Stir.

Ranch dressing and dip mix
1 pouch (28 g)

❶

Smoked paprika
15 ml (1 tbsp)

❷

Shallots
cut into wedges
125 ml (½ cup)

❸

Pork
8 loin chops
90 g (about 3 ¼ oz)
each

❹

Brussels sprouts
300 g (⅔ lb)
cut in half

❺

ALSO NEEDED:
➤ Olive oil
30 ml (2 tbsp)

Ranch Pork Chops

Prep time: **15 minutes** • Cook time: **30 minutes** • Serves: 4

Preparation

In a bowl, mix the oil, ranch dressing and dip mix, smoked paprika and shallots. Season with salt and pepper.

Transfer the oil preparation to a large freezer bag. Add the pork chops and Brussels sprouts. Close the bag and shake until the pork chops and vegetables are fully coated with the oil.

Remove the air from the bag and seal it.

Place the bag flat in the freezer.

The night before your meal, let the bag thaw out in the refrigerator.

When ready to cook, preheat the oven to 205°C (400°F).

Spread all the ingredients on a baking sheet. Bake for 30 to 35 minutes.

PER SERVING	
Calories	363
Protein	42 g
Fat	15 g
Carbohydrates	15 g
Fibre	4 g
Iron	3 mg
Calcium	151 mg
Sodium	503 mg

Good to Know

The many beneficial properties of Brussels sprouts

The Brussels sprout is small but mighty when it comes to nutritional qualities: it's rich in vitamin C, potassium and folic acid, and it's high in fibre too. Just like its close relations in the cruciferous family (cabbage, turnip, etc.) or spinach, it's packed with antioxidants, which effectively protect against several diseases and cancers. Roast them in the oven like in this recipe, enjoy crunchy slices in salads, or add them to gratins or slow-cooked stews!

Honey ❶
180 ml (¾ cup)

Soy sauce ❷
60 ml (¼ cup)

Ketchup ❸
80 ml (⅓ cup)

Chicken ❹
4 skinless breasts
sliced

**Frozen stir-fry
vegetable mix ❺**
600 g (about 1 ½ lb)

ALSO NEEDED:
➤ **Sesame oil**
(not toasted)
30 ml (2 tbsp)

➤ **Garlic**
minced
15 ml (1 tbsp)

Honey Sesame Chicken

Prep time: **15 minutes** • Cook time: **7 minutes** • Serves: **4**

Preparation

In a large bowl, mix the honey, soy sauce, ketchup, sesame oil and garlic. Season with salt and pepper.

Place the chicken in a large freezer bag. Pour a third of the sauce into the bag. Close the bag and shake until the chicken is fully coated with the sauce. Remove the air from the bag and seal it.

Pour the rest of the sauce into another freezer bag. Close the bag, then remove the air and seal it.

Place the bags flat in the freezer.

The night before your meal, let the bags thaw out in the refrigerator.

When ready to cook, drain the chicken and discard the sauce.

Heat a little canola oil in a large frying pan or wok over medium heat. Cook the chicken for 4 to 5 minutes, turning the slices halfway through cooking time, until it's no longer pink in the center.

Add the vegetables and cook for 2 to 3 minutes, stirring.

Pour the sauce from the second bag into the pan and bring to a boil. Cook for 1 to 2 minutes, stirring.

PER SERVING	
Calories	559
Protein	45 g
Fat	13 g
Carbohydrates	69 g
Fibre	4 g
Iron	2 mg
Calcium	55 mg
Sodium	900 mg

Learn More

Honey

Whether it's locally produced or imported from elsewhere, honey has some surprising properties. It's a major source of flavonoids, antioxidants that help prevent certain cancers, cardiovascular diseases and neurodegenerative diseases. Honey has also long been known as a popular home remedy due to its healing and antiseptic properties. Bees work no less than 7,000 hours to produce 500 g (about 1 ½ cups) of honey!

Pork ❶
8 loin chops
60 g (about
2 ¼ oz) each
cut into strips

**Peanut
cooking sauce** ❷
250 ml (1 cup)

1 small red onion ❸
diced

Bell peppers ❹
½ green and ½ red
chopped

Sugar snap peas ❺
100 g (3 ½ oz)

ALSO NEEDED:
➤ **Garlic**
minced
5 ml (1 tsp)

OPTIONAL:
➤ **Mint**
a few leaves

Peanut Pork Stir-fry

Prep time: **15 minutes** • Cook time: **6 minutes** • Serves: **4**

Preparation

Place the pork strips in a large freezer bag and pour in the sauce. Close the bag and shake until the pork strips are fully coated with the sauce. Remove the air from the bag and seal it.

Place the red onion, bell peppers, sugar snap peas and garlic in another large freezer bag. Remove the air from the bag and seal it.

Place the bags flat in the freezer.

The night before your meal, let the bags thaw out in the refrigerator.

When ready to cook, drain the pork strips, keeping the sauce.

Heat a little canola oil in a frying pan over medium heat. Cook the pork strips for 2 minutes on each side. Remove from the pan and set aside on a plate.

In the same pan, cook the vegetables for 4 to 5 minutes, stirring a few times. Remove the vegetables from the pan and set aside on a plate.

Pour the sauce in the pan and bring to a boil. Place the pork strips and vegetables back into the pan. Bring to a boil again.

Sprinkle with mint leaves before serving, if desired.

PER SERVING	
Calories	349
Protein	29 g
Fat	16 g
Carbohydrates	25 g
Fibre	2 g
Iron	2 mg
Calcium	33 mg
Sodium	566 mg

Homemade Version

Peanut sauce

In a bowl, mix 250 ml (1 cup) chicken stock, 60 ml (¼ cup) crunchy peanut butter, 80 ml (⅓ cup) chopped unsalted peanuts, 30 ml (2 tbsp) soy sauce and 5 ml (1 tsp) curry. Season with salt and pepper.

Pineapple ①
cut into small pieces
1 can (398 ml)

Honey ②
15 ml (1 tbsp)

24 medium shrimp ③
(31-40 count)
raw and peeled

3 bell pepper halves ④
various colours
diced

16 sugar snap peas ⑤

ALSO NEEDED:
➤ **½ red onion**
diced

OPTIONAL:
➤ **Lime zest**
15 ml (1 tbsp)

Pineapple-glazed Shrimp

Prep time: **15 minutes** • Cook time: **7 minutes** • Serves: **4**

Preparation

In a bowl, pour the pineapple juice from the can. Add the honey, shrimp and lime zest, if desired. Stir.

Place the shrimp and sauce in a large freezer bag. Close the bag and shake until the shrimp are fully coated with the sauce. Remove the air from the bag and seal it.

Place the pineapple, bell peppers, sugar snap peas and red onion in another large freezer bag. Remove the air from the bag and seal it.

Place the bags flat in the freezer.

The night before your meal, let the bags thaw out in the refrigerator.

When ready to cook, drain the shrimp, keeping the sauce.

Heat a little canola oil in a frying pan over medium heat. Cook the shrimp for 2 minutes on each side. Set aside on a plate.

In the same frying pan, cook the pineapple and vegetable mix for 3 to 4 minutes.

Put the rest of the marinade and shrimp back into the pan. Cook for 2 to 3 minutes, until the shrimp caramelize.

PER SERVING	
Calories	208
Protein	17 g
Fat	3 g
Carbohydrates	28 g
Fibre	2 g
Iron	3 mg
Calcium	73 mg
Sodium	120 mg

Side Dish Idea

Almond milk rice

Rinse 125 ml (½ cup) jasmine rice with cold water. Place in a pot with 200 ml (¾ cup + 4 tsp) almond milk, 125 ml (½ cup) water and a pinch of salt. Bring to a boil. Cover and cook over medium-low heat for 20 to 25 minutes, stirring from time to time, until the rice is cooked.

Red curry paste ①
30 ml (2 tbsp)

Garam masala ②
5 ml (1 tsp)

4 tomatoes ③
diced

Coconut milk ④
1 can (398 ml)

Chicken ⑤
4 skinless breasts
cut into small cubes

ALSO NEEDED:
➤ **Lemon juice**
15 ml (1 tbsp)

Red Curry Chicken

Prep time: **15 minutes** • Cook time: **23 minutes** • Serves: **4**

Preparation

In a bowl, mix the red curry paste and garam masala. Add the tomatoes, coconut milk and lemon juice. Stir.

Place the cubed chicken in a large freezer bag and pour in the curry sauce. Season with salt and pepper. Close the bag and shake until the chicken is fully coated with the sauce. Remove the air from the bag and seal it.

Place the bag flat in the freezer.

The night before your meal, let the bag thaw out in the refrigerator.

When ready to cook, drain the chicken, keeping the sauce.

Heat a little canola oil in a frying pan over medium heat. Brown the chicken cubes for 3 to 4 minutes on each surface.

Pour in the sauce and bring to a boil. Let simmer for 20 to 25 minutes, until the chicken is no longer pink in the centre.

PER SERVING	
Calories	425
Protein	43 g
Fat	22 g
Carbohydrates	13 g
Fibre	4 g
Iron	3 mg
Calcium	49 mg
Sodium	656 mg

Side Dish Idea

Chapati bread

In a bowl, mix 250 ml (1 cup) whole wheat flour with 250 ml (1 cup) white flour and 2.5 ml (½ tsp) salt. Gradually add 250 ml (1 cup) water and mix until the dough forms a ball. Knead the dough for 5 minutes. Cover the bowl with a damp dish towel and let the dough set for 1 hour at room temperature. Knead the dough again for 3 minutes. Divide into 12 balls. On a floured surface, roll out each ball to form 15 cm (6 in) circles. Heat 15 ml (1 tbsp) canola oil in a frying pan over medium-low heat. Cook one chapati at a time for 1 minute, until bubbles form on the surface of the dough. Turn the chapati and cook until the bread is lightly browned. Cook the rest of the chapatis, following the same steps.

Butter chicken cooking sauce
180 ml (¾ cup)
1

Coconut milk
125 ml (½ cup)
2

Beef
sirloin
450 g (1 lb)
cut into strips
3

2 carrots
cut into thin
julienne strips
4

10 snow peas
cut into thin
julienne strips
5

OPTIONAL:
➤ Cilantro
30 ml (2 tbsp)

Butter Beef Stir-fry

Prep time: **15 minutes** • Cook time: **5 minutes** • Serves: **4**

Preparation

In a bowl, mix the butter chicken sauce with the coconut milk.

Place the beef strips in a large freezer bag and pour in the sauce. Season with salt and pepper. Close the bag and shake until the beef is fully coated with the sauce. Remove the air from the bag and seal it.

Place the carrots and snow peas in another large freezer bag. Remove the air from the bag and seal it.

Place the bags flat in the freezer.

The night before your meal, let the bags thaw out in the refrigerator.

When ready to eat, drain the beef strips, keeping the sauce.

Heat a little canola oil in a frying pan over medium heat. Cook the beef for 2 to 3 minutes, stirring. Transfer onto a plate.

Pour the sauce into the pan. Bring to a boil and simmer for 2 to 3 minutes.

Put the beef strips back into the pan and add the vegetables. Cook for 2 to 3 minutes, stirring. Sprinkle with cilantro before serving, if desired.

PER SERVING	
Calories	296
Protein	27 g
Fat	16 g
Carbohydrates	10 g
Fibre	2 g
Iron	4 mg
Calcium	47 mg
Sodium	290 mg

Side Dish Idea

Vegetable couscous

In a pot, bring 250 ml (1 cup) chicken stock to a boil. In a bowl, mix 250 ml (1 cup) couscous with 15 ml (1 tbsp) olive oil. Pour the stock into the couscous and then cover and let sit for 5 minutes. Fluff with a fork. Dice 1 zucchini, 1 red bell pepper and 1 small onion. Heat 15 ml (1 tbsp) olive oil in a frying pan over medium-high heat. Cook the vegetables for 2 to 3 minutes. Add the vegetables, 15 ml (1 tbsp) chopped basil and 5 ml (1 tsp) chopped oregano to the couscous bowl. Season with salt and pepper, and stir.

Orange juice ❶
250 ml (1 cup)

Soy sauce ❷
45 ml (3 tbsp)

Firm tofu ❸
1 block (454 g)
cut into roughly
1.5 cm (⅔ in) cubes

1 carrot ❹
cut into thin
julienne strips

6 shiitakes ❺
stems removed
and caps chopped

ALSO NEEDED:
➤ **Cornstarch**
15 ml (1 tbsp)

➤ **Garlic**
minced
10 ml (2 tsp)

➤ **Canola oil**
45 ml (3 tbsp)

OPTIONAL:
➤ **Whole water chestnuts**
drained
1 can (227 ml)

➤ **Cashew nuts**
80 ml (⅓ cup)

Orange Tofu Stir-fry

Prep time: **15 minutes** • Cook time: **6 minutes** • Serves: **4**

Preparation

In a bowl, mix the orange juice, soy sauce and cornstarch. Season with salt and pepper.

Place the tofu cubes in a large freezer bag and pour in the sauce. Close the bag and shake until the tofu is fully coated with the sauce. Remove the air from the bag and seal it.

Place the carrot, shiitakes, garlic, and water chestnuts, if desired, into another large freezer bag. Remove the air from the bag and seal it.

Place the bags flat in the freezer.

The day before your meal, let the bags thaw out in the refrigerator.

When ready to cook, drain the tofu, keeping the sauce.

Heat the oil in a large frying pan or wok over medium heat. Brown the tofu cubes for 2 to 3 minutes on each surface. Set aside on a plate.

In the same pan, cook the vegetables and cashew nuts, if desired, for 3 to 4 minutes.

Pour the sauce into the pan and bring to a boil, stirring.

Place the tofu back into the pan and heat for 1 minute, stirring.

Learn More

The many benefits of tofu

Soy, the basic ingredient of tofu, is a very high-quality source of protein. Of all the legumes, it contains the highest amount of complete protein, proteins containing all nine of the essential amino acids. This means that tofu can easily replace the meat in your meals once or twice a week. Unlike meat, it is low in saturated fat and even has good fat that helps reduce blood cholesterol levels. Tofu also contains significant amounts of phytoestrogens, which are plant hormones that are thought to help reduce the severity of menopausal symptoms. Tofu can be eaten grilled, sautéed, stir-fried or stewed. It can also be crumbled into soups and salads.

PER SERVING	
Calories	332
Protein	17 g
Fat	21 g
Carbohydrates	28 g
Fibre	4 g
Iron	8 mg
Calcium	287 mg
Sodium	708 mg

Maple syrup ❶
180 ml (¾ cup)

Apple cider vinegar ❷
30 ml (2 tbsp)

Ginger ❸
minced
15 ml (1 tbsp)

Chicken ❹
4 skinless breasts
cut into cubes

1 bell pepper ❺
orange or yellow
cut into cubes

ALSO NEEDED:
➤ Chicken stock
180 ml (¾ cup)

Maple Chicken and Bell Pepper Stir-fry

Prep time: **15 minutes** • Cook time: **14 minutes** • Serves: 4

Preparation

In a bowl, mix the maple syrup, apple cider vinegar, ginger and chicken stock.

Place the chicken breasts and pepper cubes in a large freezer bag and pour in the sauce. Season with salt and pepper. Close the bag and shake it to ensure the chicken is fully coated with the sauce. Remove the air from the bag and seal it.

Place the bag flat in the freezer.

The night before your meal, let the bag thaw out in the refrigerator.

When ready to cook, drain the chicken preparation, keeping the sauce.

Heat a little canola oil in a large frying pan over medium heat. Brown the chicken and pepper cubes for 2 to 3 minutes.

Pour the sauce into the pan. Cover and simmer for 12 to 15 minutes over medium heat, until the chicken is no longer pink in the centre.

PER SERVING	
Calories	435
Protein	41 g
Fat	10 g
Carbohydrates	45 g
Fibre	0 g
Iron	2 mg
Calcium	81 mg
Sodium	375 mg

Side Dish Idea

Rice pilaf

In a pot, melt 30 ml (2 tbsp) butter over medium heat. Add 250 ml (1 cup) long grain white rice. Stir for a few seconds to fully coat the rice with butter. Pour in 500 ml (2 cups) chicken stock and bring to a boil over medium heat. Cover and simmer for 18 to 20 minutes over low heat. When ready to serve, sprinkle with 2 green onions, chopped.

Beef stock ❶
250 ml (1 cup)

Tomato paste ❷
15 ml (1 tbsp)

Paprika ❸
10 ml (2 tsp)

6 mild Italian sausages ❹
cooked and cut
into 1 cm (½ in)
thick slices

10 mushrooms ❺
sliced

ALSO NEEDED:
➤ **1 onion**
diced
➤ **Cooking cream
(15%)**
125 ml (½ cup)

Tomato and Paprika Sausages

Prep time: **15 minutes** • Cook time: **10 minutes** • Serves: **4**

Preparation

In a bowl, mix the stock, tomato paste and paprika.

Place the sausages in a large freezer bag and pour in the sauce. Season with salt and pepper. Close the bag and shake until the sausages are fully coated with the sauce. Remove the air from the bag and seal it.

Place the onion and mushrooms in another large freezer bag. Remove the air from the bag and seal it.

Place the bags flat in the freezer.

The night before your meal, let the bags thaw out in the refrigerator.

When ready to cook, heat a little canola oil in a large frying pan over medium heat. Sauté the onion and mushrooms for 2 to 3 minutes.

Add the sausages and the sauce from the first bag. Bring to a boil and simmer over medium-low heat for 5 to 6 minutes.

Pour in the cream and cook for another 3 minutes.

PER SERVING	
Calories	547
Protein	20 g
Fat	49 g
Carbohydrates	8 g
Fibre	2 g
Iron	2 mg
Calcium	201 mg
Sodium	1,067 mg

Side Dish Idea

Thyme sugar snap peas

In a pot of boiling, salted water, cook 375 ml (1½ cups) sugar snap peas for 4 to 5 minutes. Drain and put back into the pot. Add 10 ml (2 tsp) butter, 5 ml (1 tsp) honey, 2.5 ml (½ tsp) white wine vinegar and 2.5 ml (½ tsp) chopped thyme. Season with salt and pepper, and stir.

Ginger stir-fry sauce ❶
250 ml (1 cup)

Beef ❷
2 sirloin steaks
250 g (about ½ lb) each
cut into strips

1 mango ❸
cut into strips

1 red bell pepper ❹
cut into strips

Green beans ❺
200 g (about ½ lb)
cut into pieces

ALSO NEEDED:
➤ **½ red onion**
cut into thin wedges

➤ **Sesame oil**
(not toasted)
30 ml (2 tbsp)

Beef, Mango and Pepper Stir-fry

Prep time: **15 minutes** • Cook time: **6 minutes** • Serves: **4**

Preparation

Pour the sauce into a large freezer bag and add the beef strips. Season with salt and pepper. Close the bag and shake until the beef strips are fully coated with the sauce. Remove the air from the bag and seal it.

Place the mango, pepper, beans and red onion in another large airtight bag. Remove the air from the bag and seal it.

Place the bags flat in the freezer.

The night before your meal, let the bags thaw out in the refrigerator.

When ready to cook, drain the beef strips, keeping the sauce.

Heat half of the sesame oil in a frying pan over medium heat. Season the beef with salt and pepper, then cook the strips for 2 to 3 minutes on each side. Remove from the pan and set aside.

Heat the rest of the oil in the same pan over medium heat. Cook the mango, pepper, red onion and beans for 2 minutes.

Add the beef strips and sauce to the pan. Bring to a boil.

PER SERVING	
Calories	455
Protein	32 g
Fat	14 g
Carbohydrates	16 g
Fibre	5 g
Iron	6 mg
Calcium	61 mg
Sodium	1,082 mg

Homemade Version

Lemon ginger sauce

In a pot, place 10 ml (2 tsp) minced garlic, 15 ml (1 tbsp) minced ginger, 15 ml (1 tbsp) lemon zest, 15 ml (1 tbsp) rice vinegar, 15 ml (1 tbsp) sesame seeds, 15 ml (1 tbsp) corn-starch, 30 ml (2 tbsp) soy sauce, 30 ml (2 tbsp) honey, 375 ml (1 ½ cups) beef stock and ½ of a Thai pepper, chopped. Stir. Bring to a boil. Remove from the heat and let cool.

Lime juice ①
30 ml (2 tbsp)

Fish sauce ②
15 ml (1 tbsp)

Soy sauce ③
low sodium
15 ml (1 tbsp)

Brown sugar ④
15 ml (1 tbsp)

Mix of frozen shrimp ⑤
and scallops
2 bags (340 g each)

ALSO NEEDED:
➤ **Garlic**
   minced
   10 ml (2 tsp)
➤ **1 onion**
   diced

OPTIONAL:
➤ **Hot pepper**
   finely chopped
   to taste
➤ **Cilantro**
   30 ml (2 tbsp)

Seafood Stir-fry

Prep time: **15 minutes** • Cook time: **5 minutes** • Serves: **4**

Preparation

In a bowl, mix the lime juice with the fish sauce, soy sauce and brown sugar.

Pour the sauce in a large freezer bag. Add the garlic, onion, and hot pepper, if desired. Season with salt and pepper. Close the bag and shake it to fully coat the ingredients with the sauce. Remove the air from the bag and seal it.

Place the bag flat in the freezer.

The night before your meal, let the vegetable and seafood bags thaw out in the refrigerator.

When ready to cook, heat a little sesame oil (not toasted) or canola oil in a large frying pan or wok over medium heat. Cook the shrimp and scallop mix for 1 to 2 minutes on each side. Remove from the pan and set aside on a plate.

In the same pan, cook the prepared vegetables for 1 to 2 minutes.

Put the seafood back into the pan and cook for 2 to 3 minutes, stirring.

Divide the seafood onto plates. Sprinkle each serving with cilantro, if desired.

PER SERVING	
Calories	120
Protein	22 g
Fat	1 g
Carbohydrates	10 g
Fibre	1 g
Iron	0 mg
Calcium	56 mg
Sodium	1,357 mg

Side Dish Idea

Sesame stir-fried rice noodles

Soak 200 g (about ½ lb) large rice noodles according to the instructions on the packaging. Drain. Heat 30 ml (2 tbsp) sesame oil (not toasted) in a pot over medium heat. Cook the rice noodles for 1 to 2 minutes, stirring. Add 15 ml (1 tbsp) roasted sesame seeds and 60 ml (¼ cup) green onions. Season with salt and pepper, and stir.

Teriyaki sauce ①
low sodium
250 ml (1 cup)

Chicken ②
3 skinless breasts
sliced

Broccoli ③
cut into small florets
250 ml (1 cup)

1 red bell pepper ④
diced

Thai basil ⑤
60 ml (¼ cup)
of leaves

ALSO NEEDED:
➤ **1 onion**
diced
➤ **Sesame oil**
(not toasted)
30 ml (2 tbsp)

OPTIONAL:
➤ **Snow peas**
250 ml (1 cup)

Chicken and Thai Basil Stir-fry

Prep time: **15 minutes** • Cook time: **9 minutes** • Serves: **4**

Preparation

Pour the teriyaki sauce into a large freezer bag. Add the chicken strips. Close the bag and shake until the chicken is fully coated with the sauce. Remove the air from the bag and seal it.

Place the broccoli, bell pepper, onion, and snow peas, if desired, in another large freezer bag. Remove the air from the bag and seal it.

Place the bags flat in the freezer.

The night before your meal, let the bags thaw out in the refrigerator.

When ready to cook, drain the prepared chicken, keeping the sauce.

Heat half of the sesame oil in a large frying pan or wok over medium heat. Sear the chicken strips for 2 to 3 minutes, working in small batches, until they are no longer pink in the centre. Transfer to a plate.

Clean out the frying pan and then heat the rest of the sesame oil over medium heat. Cook the vegetables for 2 to 3 minutes.

Return the chicken to the frying pan and add the basil leaves and sauce. Bring to a boil, stirring. Cook over low heat for 5 to 6 minutes.

PER SERVING	
Calories	313
Protein	36 g
Fat	9 g
Carbohydrates	21 g
Fibre	2 g
Iron	1 mg
Calcium	40 mg
Sodium	1,415 mg

Homemade Version

Asian stir-fry sauce

In a bowl, mix 250 ml (1 cup) chicken stock, 30 ml (2 tbsp) soy sauce, 30 ml (2 tbsp) yellow curry paste, 15 ml (1 tbsp) fish sauce, 15 ml (1 tbsp) brown sugar and 10 ml (2 tsp) cornstarch.

Brussels sprouts ①
350 g (about ¾ lb)

1 small red onion ②
diced

1 red bell pepper ③
diced

Garlic ④
minced
10 ml (2 tsp)

30 jumbo shrimp ⑤
(21-25 count)
frozen and peeled

OPTIONAL:
➤ **2 limes**
cut into slices

Shrimp and Brussels Sprout Stir-fry

Prep time: **15 minutes** • Cook time: **10 minutes** • Serves: **4**

Preparation

In a pot of boiling, salted water, blanch the Brussels sprouts for 3 to 4 minutes. Rinse under cold water and then drain. Cut the Brussels sprouts in half.

Place the red onion, bell pepper, garlic and Brussels sprouts in a large freezer bag. Remove the air from the bag and seal it.

Place the bag flat in the freezer.

The night before your meal, let the bag and the shrimp thaw out in the refrigerator.

When ready to cook, melt a little butter in a frying pan over medium heat. Cook the shrimp for 1 to 2 minutes on each side. Transfer onto a plate.

In the same pan, cook the vegetables for 4 to 6 minutes, stirring. Season with salt and pepper.

Add the shrimp and heat for 1 minute. Serve with the sliced lime, if desired.

PER SERVING	
Calories	212
Protein	15 g
Fat	11 g
Carbohydrates	18 g
Fibre	5 g
Iron	3 mg
Calcium	90 mg
Sodium	147 mg

Good To Know

Buying shrimp by the count

Shrimp are available in several sizes, but what do the numbers 16-20 or 31-40 on the packaging actually mean? These two different numbers simply correspond to the number of shrimp per pound. The lower the number, the bigger the shrimp, and vice-versa.

- **Colossal** shrimp (8-12 and 13-15) and **jumbo shrimp** (from 16-20 to 26-30) can be grilled on the barbecue or cooked in the oven or on the stovetop.

- **Medium shrimp** (from 31-40 to 51-60) are perfect in salads, soups, stir-fries and pastas.

- **Small shrimp** (from 61-70 to 90-110) are great for appetizers and verrines.

Pork and Vegetable Fried Rice

Prep time: **15 minutes** • Cook time: **6 minutes** • Serves: **4**

Soy sauce ❶
low sodium
60 ml (¼ cup)

Rice vinegar ❷
45 ml (3 tbsp)

Pork ❸
450 g (1 lb)
of loin chops
diced

Rice ❹
cooked
1 litre (4 cups)

**Frozen stir-fry
vegetable mix** ❺
300 g (⅓ lb)

ALSO NEEDED:
➤ **Sugar**
10 ml (2 tsp)

OPTIONAL:
➤ **Frozen green peas**
250 ml (1 cup)
➤ **3 eggs**
beaten

Preparation

In a bowl, mix the soy sauce, rice vinegar and sugar.

Transfer the sauce to a large freezer bag. Add the diced pork and shake until it is fully coated with the sauce. Remove the air from the bag and seal it.

Place the cooked rice in another large freezer bag. Remove the air from the bag and seal it.

Place the bags flat in the freezer.

The night before your meal, let the bags, frozen vegetables, and green peas, if desired, thaw out in the refrigerator.

When ready to cook, drain the pork, keeping the sauce. Use a colander to drain the mixed vegetables and green peas, if using.

Heat a little canola oil in a frying pan over medium heat. Cook the diced pork for 3 to 4 minutes.

Add the vegetables. Cook for 3 to 4 minutes. Set aside on a plate.

Pour the eggs into the same frying pan and stir until they are cooked through, if desired. Break them up into small pieces.

Return the pork and vegetables to the pan. Add the rice and reheat for 2 minutes, stirring.

Pour in the sauce and cook for 1 minute, stirring.

PER SERVING	
Calories	587
Protein	37 g
Fat	16 g
Carbohydrates	71 g
Fibre	4 g
Iron	3 mg
Calcium	70 mg
Sodium	688 mg

Learn More

Cantonese fried rice

What makes Cantonese rice different from other fried rice dishes? It's the addition of an egg, which is fried at the same time as the rice. This means that if you choose to add the eggs to the recipe, you'll be serving up this popular Asian dish! Cantonese rice is traditionally prepared with pork and a mix of vegetables, most often green peas and carrots.

Orange juice
250 ml (1 cup) **1**

Turmeric **2**
2.5 ml (½ tsp)

Honey **3**
30 ml (2 tbsp)

Chicken **4**
12 thighs
bones and skin
removed
cut into pieces

12 small **5**
asparagus
cut into 2.5 cm
(1 in) pieces

Orange and Asparagus Chicken Stir-fry

Prep time: **15 minutes** •Cook time: **6 minutes** • Serves: **6**

Preparation

In a large freezer bag, place the orange juice, turmeric and honey. Close the bag and shake to mix. Remove the air from the bag and seal it.

Place the chicken thighs in another large freezer bag. Remove the air from the bag and seal it.

Place the asparagus and red onion in a third large freezer bag. Remove the air from the bag and seal it.

Place the bags flat in the freezer.

The night before your meal, let the bags thaw out in the refrigerator.

When ready to cook, heat a little canola oil in a large frying pan or wok over medium heat. Cook the chicken thighs for 5 to 6 minutes, until the chicken is no longer pink in the centre, turning them over halfway through cooking.

Add the asparagus and onion and cook for 1 to 2 minutes, stirring.

Add the orange juice sauce. Season with salt and pepper, and bring to a boil.

Dissolve the cornstarch in a little cold water and add to the pan. Simmer for 1 minute over low heat, stirring.

Sprinkle with green onions and cilantro leaves before serving, if desired.

PER SERVING	
Calories	247
Protein	23 g
Fat	11 g
Carbohydrates	15 g
Fibre	1 g
Iron	2 mg
Calcium	28 mg
Sodium	104 mg

Side Dish Idea

Zucchini rice noodles

Soak the contents of 1 pack of rice noodles (250 g) according to the instructions on the packaging. Drain. Heat 30 ml (2 tbsp) peanut oil in a frying pan over medium heat. Brown 1 chopped onion for 1 minute. Add 2 diced zucchinis and cook for 2 minutes. Add the noodles and 30 ml (2 tbsp) sesame seeds. Heat for 1 minute.

ALSO NEEDED:
➤ **1 small red onion**
diced

➤ **Cornstarch**
10 ml (2 tsp)

OPTIONAL:
➤ **2 green onions**
chopped

➤ **Cilantro**
30 ml (2 tbsp)

1 red bell pepper
cut into cubes
❶

Cauliflower
cut into small florets
375 ml (1 ½ cups)
❷

Coconut milk
1 can (400 ml)
❸

Curry paste
30 ml (2 tbsp)
❹

Salmon
fillets, 2 cm (¾ in) thick
600 g (about 1 ⅓ lb)
skin removed and cut
into cubes
❺

Salmon and Vegetable Curry

Prep time: **15 minutes** • Cook time: **12 minutes** • Serves: **4**

Preparation

Place the bell pepper, cauliflower, onion, and snow peas, if desired, in a large freezer bag. Remove the air from the bag and seal it.

Place the curry paste and coconut milk in a second large freezer bag. Close the bag and shake to mix. Remove the air from the bag and seal it.

Place the salmon cubes in a third large freezer bag. Remove the air from the bag and seal it.

Place the bags flat in the freezer.

The night before your meal, let the bags thaw out in the refrigerator.

When ready to cook, heat a little canola oil in a large frying pan over medium heat. Cook the vegetables for 2 to 3 minutes.

Add the coconut milk and curry paste. Bring to a boil and simmer for 5 minutes over medium-low heat.

Add the salmon cubes and stir. Bring to a boil again. Cover and simmer for 4 to 5 minutes over low heat, until the salmon is cooked through.

Learn More

Curry

Curry is a blend of spices that are commonly used in India, similar to masala, another spice blend. What makes up these blends varies by region: ginger, garlic, cardamom, cumin, turmeric, black pepper, chili pepper, fenugreek–the list is long and varied! The word curry comes from the time of colonial British rule in India, when the British called the stewed dishes prepared for them by their Indian chef "curries," and has come to refer to both the spice blend and the dish. Curry paste is a very concentrated mixture of spices that also contains aromatic herbs.

PER SERVING	
Calories	600
Protein	35 g
Fat	43 g
Carbohydrates	13 g
Fibre	3 g
Iron	3 mg
Calcium	70 mg
Sodium	196 mg

ALSO NEEDED:
➤ **1 onion**
chopped

OPTIONAL:
➤ **Snow peas**
150 g (⅓ lb)

Teriyaki sauce ①
180 ml (¾ cup)

Extra firm tofu ②
cut into cubes
1 block (350 g)

3 ½ bell peppers ③
various colours
cut into cubes

1 zucchini ④
cut into half rounds

Sugar snap peas ⑤
100 g (3 ½ oz)

Teriyaki Tofu Stir-fry

Prep time: **15 minutes** • Cook time: **6 minutes** • Serves: 4

Preparation

In a large freezer bag, place the teriyaki sauce, tofu, and lemongrass, if desired. Close the bag and shake until the tofu is fully coated with the sauce. Remove the air from the bag and seal it.

Place the bell peppers, zucchini, sugar snap peas, red onion, and mushrooms, if desired, in another large freezer bag. Remove the air from the bag and seal it.

Place the bags flat in the freezer.

The night before your meal, let the bags thaw out in the refrigerator.

When ready to cook, heat a little canola oil in a large frying pan or wok over medium heat. Cook the vegetables for 3 to 4 minutes over medium heat. Transfer onto a plate.

In the same pan, bring the tofu cubes and the sauce to a boil over medium heat. Simmer for 2 to 3 minutes.

Put the vegetables back into the pan and heat for 1 to 2 minutes, stirring.

PER SERVING	
Calories	295
Protein	16 g
Fat	8 g
Carbohydrates	48 g
Fibre	6 g
Iron	6 mg
Calcium	239 mg
Sodium	695 mg

Homemade Version

Teriyaki sauce

In a bowl, mix 125 ml (½ cup) soy sauce, 125 ml (½ cup) chicken stock, 45 ml (3 tbsp) mirin and 5 ml (1 tsp) minced garlic.

OPTIONAL:
➤ **Lemongrass**
1 stalk, white part
chopped

➤ **Mushrooms**
sliced
1 container (227 g)

ALSO NEEDED:
➤ **1 small red onion**
cut into cubes

Pork ①
1 tenderloin
600 g (about 1 ⅓ lb)
trimmed and cut
into strips

**Honey garlic
marinade** ②
125 ml (½ cup)

1 small red onion ③

**Frozen stir-fry
vegetable mix** ④
500 ml (2 cups)

Sweet chili sauce ⑤
375 ml (1 ½ cups)

OPTIONAL:
➤ **Ginger**
minced
15 ml (1 tbsp)

Asian-style Pork
and Vegetable Stir-fry

Prep time: **15 minutes** • Cook time: **10 minutes** • Serves: **4**

Preparation

Place the pork strips and marinade in a large freezer
bag. Close the bag and shake until the pork is fully
coated in the marinade. Remove the air from the bag
and seal it.

Place the red onion, mixed vegetables, and ginger,
if desired, in another large freezer bag.

Place the bags flat in the freezer.

The night before your meal, let the bags thaw out
in the refrigerator.

When ready to cook, drain the pork strips and discard
the marinade.

Heat a little canola oil in a frying pan over medium heat.
Cook the pork strips for 2 to 3 minutes, working in small
batches. Set aside on a plate.

In the same frying pan, cook the vegetables for
3 minutes, stirring, until tender.

Pour in the chili sauce and bring to a boil. Return the
pork strips to the pan and reheat for 1 to 2 minutes.

PER SERVING	
Calories	455
Protein	35 g
Fat	5 g
Carbohydrates	61 g
Fibre	2 g
Iron	2 mg
Calcium	37 mg
Sodium	1,333 mg

Learn More

Ginger

Ginger is a root that comes from Southeast Asia and has always
been known for its medicinal and aromatic properties. Some would
even call it an aphrodisiac! Frequently used in Asian cuisines, ginger
adds a kick to savoury dishes like this one, as well as sweet treats.
You can find it at the supermarket in fresh, pickled or powdered
forms. Fresh ginger keeps for two to three weeks in the refrigerator,
but it can also be frozen, either as is or peeled and cut into chunks,
for up to a year!

Mango curry sauce ①
375 ml (1 ½ cups)

3 parsnips ②
peeled and
cut into sticks

Baby carrots ③
450 g (1 lb)

Chicken ④
4 skinless breasts
cut into cubes

Rice ⑤
cooked
1 litre (4 cups)

OPTIONAL:
➤ **Cilantro**
a few leaves

Mango Curry Chicken

Prep time: **15 minutes** • Cook time: **11 minutes** • Serves: **4**

Preparation

Pour the sauce into a large freezer bag. Add the parsnips and baby carrots. Close the bag and shake until the vegetables are fully coated with the sauce. Remove the air from the bag and seal it.

Place the chicken cubes in a second large freezer bag. Remove the air from the bag and seal it.

Place the cooked rice in a third large freezer bag. Remove the air from the bag and seal it.

Place the bags flat in the freezer.

The night before your meal, let the bags thaw out in the refrigerator.

When ready to cook, heat a little canola oil in a frying pan over medium heat. Cook the chicken cubes for 5 to 6 minutes, until the meat is no longer pink in the center.

Add the vegetables and sauce. Bring to a boil, then simmer for 6 to 8 minutes over low heat.

Place the rice in a microwave-safe bowl and reheat it in the microwave.

Divide the rice onto plates, and top with the stir-fry. Garnish with cilantro, if desired.

PER SERVING	
Calories	590
Protein	47 g
Fat	8 g
Carbohydrates	79 g
Fibre	7 g
Iron	3 mg
Calcium	92 mg
Sodium	553 mg

Homemade Version

Mango sauce

In a bowl, mix the content of 1 can of concentrated mango juice (295 ml), 125 ml (½ cup) chicken stock, 60 ml (¼ cup) soy sauce, 45 ml (3 tbsp) brown sugar, 45 ml (3 tbsp) rice vinegar, 15 ml (1 tbsp) minced ginger, 15 ml (1 tbsp) minced garlic and 2 chopped onions. Season with salt and pepper.

Main Dishes

Apple and Maple Pork Stew **208**

BBQ Chicken Pizza **276**

Beef Pizza Pockets **222**

Beef, Spinach and Ricotta Gratin **272**

Chicken Alfredo **270**

Chicken and Rice Soup **220**

Chicken and Vegetable Gratin **300**

Chicken Cannelloni **294**

Chicken, Bell Pepper and Olive Stew **194**

Chorizo and Ricotta Pasta Bake **290**

Cider Pork Roast **192**

Crab cakes **224**

Creamy Chicken and Brown Rice Gratin **262**

Creamy Chicken Pasta **226**

Creamy Fish Chowder **188**

Creamy Mushroom Sole **216**

Deluxe Homemade Pizza **298**

Easy Shepherd's Pie **256**

Hungarian Veal **206**

Indian-style Beef **190**

Italian Sole Fillets **274**

Italian-style Beef **212**

Italian-style Sausages **200**

Lemon Parmesan Chicken **282**

Lentil and Coconut Curry **198**

Light Fettuccine Alfredo **234**

Margherita Pizza **266**

Marinara Sauce Spaghetti **250**

Meatloaf **196**

Mini Chicken Cilantro Croquettes **248**

Mini Maple Tourtieres **252**

Mini Salmon and Shrimp Pies **258**

Pork and Cranberry Stew **214**

Pork and Ratatouille Noodles **242**

Quiche Lorraine **254**

Quick Chicken Pot Pie **246**

Ravioli and Zucchini Lasagna **286**

Red Wine Beef Stew **184**

Red Wine Chicken **204**

Salmon and Pancetta Quiche **244**

Salmon Cannelloni **264**

Salmon Lasagna **288**

Salmon Potato Gratin **280**

Salmon Wellington **236**

Sausage-stuffed Mini Peppers **268**

Shrimp and Pesto Stromboli **228**

Shrimp, Scallop and Cauliflower Gratin **292**

Sole Croquettes **232**

Squash and Ham Gratin **278**

Taco Casserole **296**

Texan Beef Stew **218**

Tilapia Milanese **260**

Tomato, Lentil and Chickpea Hearty Soup **210**

Tuna and Vegetable Casserole **240**

Unstuffed Cabbage Rolls **230**

Vegetable Beef Soup **202**

Vegetarian Burritos **238**

White Chili **186**

Zucchini Gratin **284**

Side Dishes

Bean, Tomato and Mozzarella Salad **216**

Caper Tartar Sauce **260**

Creamy White Wine and Parmesan Sauce **236**

Fresh Salad **288**

Garlic Mashed Potatoes **212**

Green Bean and Cherry Tomato Salad **282**

Herbed Tartar Sauce **224**

Lemon and Mint Yogurt Sauce **232**

Lemon Parsley Farfalle **292**

Marinara Sauce **274**

Mashed Potatoes **256**

Oregano Rice **204**

Parmesan Roasted Potatoes **200**

Pecan and Arugula Salad **254**

Salsa **238**

Savoury Apple Gravy **192**

Seasoned Oven Fries **298**

Sharp Cheddar Croutons **188**

Tomato and Thai Chili Pepper Garnish **210**

Yogurt, Lime and Chive Sauce **248**

From Freezer to Table

From Freezer to Table

Freezing food is an easy time-saver, but it's important to do it right. With these basic guidelines, we'll take you from preparation to freezing, with some thoughts on the best way to wrap food so you can get the most out of your freezer!

By Marie-Pier Marceau

For optimal food preservation, the freezer should be at a temperature of -18°C (0°F). Your food won't keep as well at a higher temperature, and a lower temperature would make no difference other than the waste of energy generated by the freezer. The temperature of the freezer compartments in refrigerators usually ranges from -4°C (about 25°F) to -12°C (about 10°F), which means it should be used to freeze food for short periods of time only. Chest freezers are usually kept at the correct temperature, -18°C (0°F), allowing for better long-term preservation of food–and these models can hold more too!

Don't put warm dishes in the freezer! They can raise the overall temperature of the freezer and affect the preservation of the other food inside.

Choose quality packaging

Fresh meat, poultry and fish wrapped at the supermarket keep for only a few days in the refrigerator. Freezing these items prevents them from spoiling too quickly, but they should first be transferred to a proper bag or container. That way, they'll be better protected from the cold and can be preserved longer. Make this transfer part of the process of unpacking your groceries so that you don't forget. You can even take the opportunity to add a marinade, ensuring you always have flavourful meat on hand.

For first-rate frozen veggies

Some vegetables do best in the freezer when they've been blanched first. This step stops enzyme activity, kills bacteria and helps preserve the colour, taste and texture of the vegetables. Blanch zucchini, broccoli, carrots, cauliflower and green beans for 3 minutes in boiling water. Then plunge the vegetables into a bath of very cold water to stop the cooking process. Dry them before placing them in freezer bags or containers.

Thawing 101

There are a few effective techniques for thawing out frozen food. You can take it out of the freezer the night before your meal and let it thaw out in the refrigerator. But if you forget, it's also possible to thaw out ingredients in just a few minutes by placing them in a bowl of cold water—a trick that works particularly well for shrimp! And when you're really pressed for time, the microwave is always an option, but it's important to fully cook the food as soon as you remove it from the micro-wave. Most importantly, avoid thawing out food at room temperature, as it promotes the growth of bacteria on the surface.

Well labelled, well organized!

Before storing dishes, prepped ingredients and other goodies in the freezer, take a minute to label them. Use a permanent marker on freezer bags and stickers on reusable containers, and record the date the food was prepared. Proper labelling makes it easy to keep track of what's in the freezer!

Keep your freezer clutter-free

If you use your freezer a lot, it can become jam-packed before you know it. Not only does this make it harder to remember what's inside, it also prevents the cold air from circulating properly. Try to sort through it at least once a month! Move the newer ingredients and dishes to the back and take out anything that's been frozen for a while: these items should be cooked or reheated in the next couple of days.

Check out how long your favourite foods can be frozen on page 15!

It can be frozen, but...

While most foods can be frozen, the taste, appearance or texture of some can be changed by time spent in the freezer, like these.

FOOD	WHY?
Sour cream	Becomes liquid
Fresh cheese (ricotta, cottage cheese, etc.)	Becomes grainy or liquid
Soft cheese (Brie, Camembert, etc.)	Texture changes, but can be used in sauces
Milk and 10%, 15% and 35% cream	Separates when thawed, but can be stirred to reverse the effect; thawed 35% cream can no longer be whipped
Mayonnaise	Separates
Cooked egg	Becomes rubbery and hard
Potato in soups and stews	Absorbs water and falls apart when cooked
Sauce bound with cornstarch	Separates, but the initial texture can be recovered if reheated while stirring vigorously

Shrimp photo: Shutterstock.

Beef 1
shoulder roast
600 g (about 1 ⅓ lb)
cut into cubes

4 carrots 2
cut into pieces

Red wine 3
125 ml (½ cup)

Beef stock 4
250 ml (1 cup)

Thyme 5
chopped
5 ml (1 tsp)

ALSO NEEDED:
➤ **4 onions**
sliced into rings
➤ **Flour**
15 ml (1 tbsp)

OPTIONAL:
➤ **Garlic**
minced
15 ml (1 tbsp)
➤ **1 bay leaf**

Red Wine Beef Stew

Prep time: **15 minutes** • Cook time: **2 hours 30 minutes** • Serves: 4

Preparation

Heat a cast iron casserole dish or a heavy-bottomed pot over medium heat. Sear the beef on all sides for 5 to 7 minutes, until the meat is browned.

Add the carrots and onions. Cook for another 2 to 3 minutes, stirring.

Add the garlic, if desired. Sprinkle with flour. Cook for another minute, stirring.

Pour the red wine in and stir. Simmer until almost all of the liquid has cooked down.

Add the stock, thyme, and bay leaf, if desired. Season with salt and pepper, and stir. Cover and simmer over low heat for 2 hours and 30 minutes to 3 hours, until the meat is tender.

Put the braised beef into airtight containers. Let the containers cool slightly on the counter, then refrigerate to cool completely.

Place the containers in the freezer.

The night before your meal, let the braised beef thaw out in the refrigerator.

When ready to eat, reheat the braised beef in a pot or the microwave.

Chef's Secret

Choose a good cooking wine

To ensure that your sauce tastes as it should, use a good wine. The term "good" here indicates decent quality, not a high quality wine. Cooking causes the alcohol to evaporate and leaves a concentration of the wine's characteristics, so less appealing elements tend to be enhanced. For example, a wine that is too oxidized or that is corked will affect the flavour of the dish. Here's our advice: taste some before cooking!

PER SERVING	
Calories	336
Protein	34 g
Fat	10 g
Carbohydrates	21 g
Fibre	4 g
Iron	4 mg
Calcium	77 mg
Sodium	367 mg

1 onion ①
chopped

Chicken ②
3 skinless breasts
diced

Chili seasoning ③
½ pouch (39 g)

Chicken stock ④
250 ml (1 cup)

White beans ⑤
rinsed and drained
2 cans (540 ml each)

OPTIONAL:
➤ **Tex-mex shredded cheese**
250 ml (1 cup)

➤ **1 avocado**
cut into small pieces

White Chili

Prep time: **15 minutes** • Cook time: **20 minutes** • Serves: **6**

Preparation

Heat a little olive oil in a pot over medium heat. Cook the onion for 1 minute.

Add the chicken and cook for 4 to 5 minutes, stirring from time to time.

Add the chili seasoning and stir. Pour the stock in and add the white beans. Bring to a boil, and simmer for 15 minutes, until the chicken is no longer pink in the centre.

Place the chili into airtight containers. Let it cool slightly on the counter, then refrigerate to cool completely. Place the containers in the freezer.

The night before your meal, let the chili thaw out in the refrigerator.

When ready to eat, reheat the chili in a pot or the microwave.

Serve the chili in bowls and garnish with cheese and avocado, if desired.

5•15 Tip

Always keep seasoning mixes on hand!

A good seasoning mix can be your best friend when it comes to adding a quick flavour boost to your meals. The chili seasoning in this recipe contains ingredients that give it a subtle Mexican taste: dried chillies, pepper, cumin, oregano, paprika, garlic and cloves. Many other types of seasoning mixes can be found at the grocery store, like mixes for pork, chicken, fajitas, Cajun food or Italian food. Stock up when they go on sale so that you always have some on hand!

PER SERVING	
Calories	457
Protein	38 g
Fat	17 g
Carbohydrates	40 g
Fibre	12 g
Iron	5 mg
Calcium	259 mg
Sodium	614 mg

Frozen diced vegetable mix
375 ml (1 ½ cups) ①

2% milk ②
750 ml (3 cups)

Chicken or vegetable stock ③
500 ml (2 cups)

Fish of your choice ④
(cod, haddock, sole, salmon) fillets, 450 g (1 lb) cut into 2 cm (¾ in) cubes

Cheddar ⑤
shredded
125 ml (½ cup)

ALSO NEEDED:
➤ **Flour**
60 ml (¼ cup)

OPTIONAL:
➤ **Paprika**
2.5 ml (½ tsp)

Creamy Fish Chowder

Prep time: **15 minutes** • Cook time: **7 minutes** • Serves: **4**

Preparation

Melt a little butter in a heavy-bottomed pot over medium heat. Add the mixed vegetables and cook for 2 to 3 minutes.

Sprinkle with flour. Gradually incorporate the milk and stock. Season with salt and pepper. Bring to a boil, stirring.

Turn down the heat, then add the fish and simmer for 5 minutes.

Add the shredded cheese.

Divide the chowder into airtight containers. Let it cool slightly on the counter, then refrigerate to cool completely.

Place the containers in the freezer.

The night before your meal, let the chowder thaw out in the refrigerator.

When ready to eat, reheat the chowder in a pot or the microwave.

Sprinkle a pinch of paprika over each portion before serving, if desired.

PER SERVING	
Calories	293
Protein	27 g
Fat	11 g
Carbohydrates	20 g
Fibre	2 g
Iron	1 mg
Calcium	374 mg
Sodium	1,025 mg

Side Dish Idea

Sharp cheddar croutons

Cut ⅓ of a baguette into slices and place them on a baking sheet lined with parchment paper. Brush the slices of bread with 15 ml (1 tbsp) olive oil. Sprinkle with 125 ml (½ cup) grated sharp cheddar. Broil for 2 to 3 minutes, until the cheese starts to brown.

Recipe by Diane Boudreault

Beef 1
750 g (about 1 ⅔ lb)
cut into cubes for
skewers

Red curry paste 2
30 ml (2 tbsp)

Coconut milk 3
1 can (400 ml)

3 tomatoes 4
diced

Ginger 5
minced
15 ml (1 tbsp)

ALSO NEEDED:
➤ **1 onion**
chopped
➤ **Turmeric**
1.25 ml (¼ tsp)

OPTIONAL:
➤ **Garlic**
minced
10 ml (2 tsp)
➤ **Cilantro**
chopped
30 ml (2 tbsp)

Indian-style Beef

Prep time: **15 minutes** • Cook time: **7 minutes** • Serves: **4**

Preparation

Heat a little canola oil in a frying pan over medium heat. Brown the beef cubes on all sides for 2 to 3 minutes. Transfer onto a plate.

In the same pan, cook the curry paste with the onion, turmeric, and garlic, if desired, for 1 minute over medium heat.

Add the coconut milk, tomatoes and ginger. Bring to a boil over medium heat, and cook for 2 minutes.

Add the beef cubes, and cilantro, if desired. Cook for 2 to 3 minutes, stirring.

Put the preparation into airtight containers. Let it cool slightly on the counter, then refrigerate to cool completely.

Place the containers in the freezer.

The night before your meal, let the preparation thaw out in the refrigerator.

When ready to eat, reheat in a frying pan or the microwave.

PER SERVING	
Calories	386
Protein	41 g
Fat	20 g
Carbohydrates	9 g
Fibre	2 g
Iron	4 mg
Calcium	22 mg
Sodium	639 mg

Healthy Choice

Turmeric, ginger and curry paste: loaded with healthy perks!

This Indian beef recipe contains ingredients that we would do well to add to our diets because of their health benefits. Turmeric is known for helping treat digestion problems and inflammatory diseases, and for helping prevent certain types of cancer. Ginger is commonly used in Chinese medicine to treat colds or the flu. It is also said to reduce nausea in addition to having anti-inflammatory and antioxidant properties. Finally, curry paste is known to relieve insomnia, constipation, bloating and rheumatism.

Pork ①
loin roast
900 g (about 2 lb)

Dijon mustard ②
30 ml (2 tbsp)

Onion soup mix ③
1 pouch (55 g)

2 carrots ④
chopped

Cider ⑤
250 ml (1 cup)

ALSO NEEDED:
➤ **Garlic**
minced
10 ml (2 tsp)

OPTIONAL:
➤ **1 bay leaf**
➤ **Thyme**
1 sprig

Cider Pork Roast

Prep time: **15 minutes** • Cook time: **40 minutes** • Serves: **4**

Preparation

Preheat the oven to 205°C (400°F).

Heat a little canola oil in an ovenproof skillet over medium heat. Sear the roast on all sides.

Brush the roast with the mustard, and then sprinkle the onion soup mix.

In the same pan, add the carrots, cider, garlic, and herbs, if desired. Season with salt and pepper. Bake for 40 to 50 minutes.

Place the roast in a large airtight container. Let it cool slightly on the counter, then refrigerate to cool completely.

Place the container in the freezer.

The night before your meal, let the roast thaw out in the refrigerator.

When ready to eat, reheat the roast in the oven or microwave.

PER SERVING	
Calories	429
Protein	52 g
Fat	14 g
Carbohydrates	21 g
Fibre	1 g
Iron	2 mg
Calcium	30 mg
Sodium	1,039 mg

Side Dish Idea

Savoury apple gravy

Heat 15 ml (1 tbsp) canola oil in a pot over medium-low heat. Cook 1 chopped onion and 3 peeled, diced apples for 8 minutes, until the apples are cooked. Pour in 180 ml (¾ cup) cooking cream (15%), 125 ml (½ cup) chicken stock and 30 ml (2 tbsp) maple syrup. Season with salt and pepper. Simmer over low heat for 6 to 8 minutes.

1 chicken ①
1.5 kg (3 ⅓ lb)
cut into 8 pieces

Bell peppers ②
2 red and 1 yellow
chopped

Tomato paste ③
60 ml (¼ cup)

Thyme ④
1 sprig

12 green olives ⑤

ALSO NEEDED:
➤ **2 onions**
chopped
➤ **Chicken stock**
375 ml (1½ cups)

OPTIONAL:
➤ **2 large tomatoes**
deseeded and cut into cubes
➤ **Prosciutto**
4 slices
diced

Chicken, Bell Pepper and Olive Stew

Prep time: **15 minutes** • Cook time: **30 minutes** • Serves: **6**

Preparation

Heat a little olive oil in a casserole dish or a heavy-bottomed pot over medium-high heat. Sear a few pieces of chicken at a time for 1 to 2 minutes, until they are browned on all sides. Place the chicken pieces on a plate.

In the casserole dish, cook the bell peppers and onions for 2 to 3 minutes over medium heat.

Add the tomato paste and thyme. Add the tomatoes and prosciutto, if desired. Put the chicken back into the casserole dish. Pour the stock in and season with salt and pepper. Bring to a boil. Cover and simmer for 30 to 40 minutes over medium-low heat, until the chicken is no longer pink in the centre and it comes apart easily with a fork.

Remove the casserole dish from the heat and add the olives.

Put the stew into airtight containers or freezer bags. Let them cool slightly on the counter, then refrigerate to cool completely. Place the containers in the freezer.

The night before your meal, let the stew thaw out in the refrigerator.

When ready to eat, reheat the stew in a pot or the microwave.

PAR PORTION	
Calories	604
Protein	37 g
Fat	43 g
Carbohydrates	16 g
Fibre	4 g
Iron	3 mg
Calcium	55 mg
Sodium	706 mg

Chef's Tip

Have your chicken cut

If the recipe you want to use calls for a chicken cut into 8 pieces (2 drumsticks, 2 thighs, 2 breasts and 2 wings), ask your butcher to cut it for you while you finish your grocery shopping. This service is offered free of charge at most supermarkets!

Medium ground beef ①
675 g (about 1 ½ lb)

2% milk ②
250 ml (1 cup)

Plain breadcrumbs ③
250 ml (1 cup)

Steak seasoning ④
30 ml (2 tbsp)

Worcestershire sauce ⑤
15 ml (1 tbsp)

ALSO NEEDED:
➤ **1 egg**
➤ **1 onion**
chopped

Meatloaf

Prep time: **15 minutes** • Cook time: **40 minutes** • Serves: **4**

Preparation

In a bowl, mix all the ingredients.

Line a loaf pan with parchment paper and place the preparation in it. Flatten the surface.

Cover the loaf pan with plastic wrap and then aluminum foil. Place the pan in the freezer.

The night before your meal, let the meatloaf thaw out in the refrigerator.

When ready to cook, preheat the oven to 205°C (400°F). Remove the aluminum foil and plastic wrap from the loaf pan.

Bake the meatloaf for 40 to 45 minutes, until it's no longer pink in the centre.

PAR PORTION	
Calories	579
Protein	40 g
Fat	32 g
Carbohydrates	32 g
Fibre	3 g
Iron	6 mg
Calcium	178 mg
Sodium	596 mg

Chef's Tip

For a tasty, tender meatloaf

A cooking thermometer can be a big help in determining whether your meatloaf is fully cooked. Simply insert it into the centre of the loaf, making sure you don't touch the bottom of the pan. For beef, veal, pork and lamb, the thermometer should read 71°C (160°F). For poultry, wait until the temperature is at 74°C (165°F). Another tip: let the meatloaf rest for 10 to 15 minutes before cutting it. This gives the juices time to redistribute throughout the loaf.

Curry powder ①
15 ml (1 tbsp)

Ginger ②
minced
15 ml (1 tbsp)

Dried red lentils ③
500 ml (2 cups)

Coconut milk ④
1 can (398 ml)

Diced tomatoes ⑤
1 can (540 ml)

ALSO NEEDED:
➤ **Shallots**
chopped
125 ml (½ cup)

➤ **Garlic**
minced
15 ml (1 tbsp)

OPTIONAL:
➤ **Thai chili pepper**
diced
to taste

➤ **Kale**
minced
500 ml (2 cups)

Lentil and Coconut Curry

Prep time: **15 minutes** • Cook time: **21 minutes** • Serves: **4**

Preparation

In a pot, heat a little olive oil over medium heat. Cook the curry, ginger, shallots, garlic and the Thai chili pepper, if desired, for 1 minute. Season with salt.

Add the lentils, coconut milk and diced tomatoes. Cover and cook for 20 to 25 minutes, stirring frequently, until the lentils are cooked.

Add the kale, if desired.

Divide the curry into airtight containers. Let it cool slightly on the counter, then refrigerate to cool completely.

Place the containers in the freezer.

The night before the meal, let the curry thaw out in the refrigerator.

When ready to eat, reheat the curry in a pot on the stove or in the microwave.

PER SERVING	
Calories	574
Protein	30 g
Fat	21 g
Carbohydrates	80 g
Fibre	14 g
Iron	12 mg
Calcium	180 mg
Sodium	272 mg

Healthy Choice

Red lentils

There are many benefits to integrating lentils into your diet: they are the easiest legumes to digest and are packed with fibre, antioxidants and iron. Red lentils cook faster than other varieties, making them the ideal choice for quick soups, stews and purees. With their delicate flavour and pleasing coral colour, they really brighten up this curry dish!

4 mild Italian sausages ①

4 tomato and basil sausages ②

Cherry tomatoes ③
300 g (⅔ lb)

Balsamic vinegar ④
30 ml (2 tbsp)

Arugula ⑤
375 ml (1 ½ cups)

ALSO NEEDED:
➤ **½ red onion**
chopped

➤ **Garlic**
minced
15 ml (1 tbsp)

OPTIONAL:
➤ **Basil**
chopped
30 ml (2 tbsp)

Italian-style Sausages

Prep time: **15 minutes** • Cook time: **8 minutes** • Serves: **8**

Preparation

Preheat the oven to 205°C (400°F).

Place the sausages in a pot filled with cold water. Bring to a boil and simmer over medium heat for 3 minutes. Drain.

In a bowl, mix the cherry tomatoes, balsamic vinegar, red onion, garlic, and basil, if desired. Season with salt and pepper.

Cut the sausages into pieces. Add the pieces to the bowl and stir.

Transfer the preparation into a baking dish. Bake for 8 to 10 minutes.

Remove the baking dish from the oven. Let it cool slightly on the counter, then refrigerate to cool completely.

Cover the baking dish with plastic wrap and then aluminum foil. Place the dish it in the freezer.

The night before your meal, let the dish thaw out in the refrigerator.

When ready to eat, remove the aluminum foil and plastic wrap. Reheat the preparation in the oven or microwave.

Garnish with arugula before serving.

PAR PORTION	
Calories	294
Protein	14 g
Fat	24 g
Carbohydrates	7 g
Fibre	1 g
Iron	2 mg
Calcium	18 mg
Sodium	776 mg

Side Dish Idea

Parmesan roasted potatoes

In a salad bowl, mix 30 ml (2 tbsp) olive oil, 10 ml (2 tsp) dry mustard and 8 whole garlic cloves. Add 450 g fingerling or creamer potatoes, 1 small red onion, chopped, and 3 sweet potatoes cut into cubes. Season with salt and pepper, and stir. Place onto a baking sheet lined with parchment paper. Bake for 25 to 30 minutes at 205°C (400°F), until the vegetables are fully roasted and tender. Sprinkle with 60 ml (¼ cup) parmesan shavings and 10 ml (2 tsp) chopped thyme before serving.

Beef ①
cubes for stew
340 g (¾ lb)

1 zucchini ②
diced

Diced tomatoes ③
1 can (540 ml)

Beef stock ④
low sodium
1.5 litre (6 cups)

California blend frozen vegetables ⑤
thawed
500 ml (2 cups)

ALSO NEEDED:
➤ **1 onion**
chopped

Vegetable Beef Soup

Prep time: **15 minutes** • Cook time: **25 minutes** • Serves: **6**

Preparation

Heat a little olive oil in a pot over medium heat. Brown the beef and onion for 3 to 4 minutes.

Add the zucchini, diced tomatoes and stock. Season with salt and pepper. Simmer, uncovered, for 20 minutes over medium heat.

Add the vegetable blend. Simmer, uncovered, for 5 minutes.

Divide the soup into airtight containers. Let it cool slightly on the counter, then refrigerate to cool completely. Place the containers in the freezer.

The night before your meal, let the soup thaw out in the refrigerator.

When ready to eat, reheat the soup in a pot or the microwave.

PER SERVING	
Calories	199
Protein	18 g
Fat	9 g
Carbohydrates	12 g
Fibre	2 g
Iron	2 mg
Calcium	57 mg
Sodium	826 mg

Mix It Up

Use different veggies

Of course, you can always make a delicious soup with mixed frozen vegetables, like these ones. But why not also take advantage of the abundance of seasonal produce available throughout the year? Sweet potatoes, squash, parsnips, turnips and beans all add colour and flavour to soups. Be bold and mix it up!

Roast gravy mix ①
1 pouch (34 g)

Red wine ②
375 ml (1 ½ cups)

Chicken stock ③
250 ml (1 cup)

Chicken ④
skinless breasts
650 g (about 1 ½ lb)
sliced

Bacon ⑤
precooked
8 slices cut into
pieces

ALSO NEEDED:
➤ **Garlic**
minced
10 ml (2 tsp)

➤ **1 onion**
chopped

OPTIONAL:
➤ **Tomato paste**
15 ml (1 tbsp)

Red Wine Chicken

Prep time: **15 minutes** • Cook time: **13 minutes** • Serves: 4

Preparation

In a pot, whisk the contents of the roast gravy mix with the red wine, stock, and tomato paste, if desired. Bring to a boil, whisking.

Heat a little canola oil in a frying pan over medium heat. Brown the chicken strips for 2 to 3 minutes on all sides.

Add the garlic and onion. Cook for 1 minute.

Pour the sauce into the pan. Cover and cook for 10 to 12 minutes over medium-low heat.

Remove from the heat and top with bacon. Transfer into airtight containers. Let it cool slightly on the counter, then refrigerate to cool completely. Place the containers in the freezer.

The night before your meal, let the containers thaw out in the refrigerator.

When ready to eat, reheat the chicken and sauce in a pot or the microwave.

PER SERVING	
Calories	332
Protein	42 g
Fat	7 g
Carbohydrates	9 g
Fibre	0 g
Iron	1 mg
Calcium	15 mg
Sodium	992 mg

Side Dish Idea

Oregano rice

Bring 250 ml (1 cup) chicken stock to a boil in a pot. Add 125 ml (½ cup) long-grain white rice. Cover and cook for 15 to 18 minutes over low heat. Add 60 ml (¼ cup) chopped green onions and 5 ml (1 tsp) chopped oregano. Season with salt and pepper, and stir well.

Veal ①
675 g (1 ½ lb)
cut into cubes for stew

2 carrots ②
sliced into rounds

3 tomatoes ③
diced

1 green bell pepper ④
diced

Paprika ⑤
30 ml (2 tbsp)

ALSO NEEDED:
➤ **1 onion**
chopped
➤ **Beef stock**
500 ml (2 cups)

OPTIONAL:
➤ **1 bay leaf**

Hungarian Veal

Prep time: **15 minutes** • Cook time: **1 hour** • Serves: **4**

Preparation

Heat a little canola oil in a large pot over medium-high heat. Brown the veal cubes for a few minutes on all sides.

Add the carrots, tomatoes, bell pepper, onion, beef stock, paprika, and bay leaf, if desired. Stir. Cover and simmer for 1 hour to 1 hour and 30 minutes over low heat.

Remove the pot from the heat. Place the preparation in airtight containers. Let it cool slightly on the counter, then refrigerate to cool completely. Place the containers in the freezer.

The night before your meal, let the preparation thaw out in the refrigerator.

When ready to eat, reheat the preparation in a pot or the microwave.

Healthy Choice

Veal

Did you know that veal contains less fat than beef? Veal meat comes from young cows at an age when the structure of the meat is different–leaner with a more tender texture and a milder taste. Cutlets, roasts, steaks and chops are the leanest veal cuts you can buy. Veal is also high in iron, zinc and B vitamins, making it a healthy option!

PER SERVING	
Calories	320
Protein	40 g
Fat	11 g
Carbohydrates	16 g
Fibre	4 g
Iron	5 mg
Calcium	53 mg
Sodium	526 mg

Pork
cubes for stew
750 g (about 1 ⅔ lb)

1

Maple syrup
125 ml (½ cup)

2

2 red Delicious apples
cut into wedges

3

**1 small butternut
squash**
cut into cubes

4

**8 to 10 Brussels
sprouts**
cut in half

5

ALSO NEEDED:
➤ **Flour**
30 ml (2 tbsp)
➤ **Chicken stock**
750 ml (3 cups)

OPTIONAL:
➤ **1 onion**
diced
➤ **Garlic**
minced
15 ml (1 tbsp)

Apple and Maple Pork Stew

Prep time: **15 minutes** • Cook time: **48 minutes** • Serves: **4**

Preparation

Heat a little olive oil in a pot over medium heat. Brown the pork cubes for 3 to 4 minutes on all sides.

Add the onion and garlic, if desired. Cook 1 minute.

Sprinkle with flour and stir. Pour in the maple syrup and chicken stock. Season with salt and pepper. Bring to a boil, then simmer for 30 minutes over medium-low heat.

Add the apples, squash and Brussels sprouts. Continue cooking for 15 to 20 minutes, until the vegetables are tender.

Remove from heat. Divide the stew into airtight containers. Let it cool slightly on the counter, then refrigerate to cool completely. Place the containers in the freezer.

The night before your meal, let the stew thaw out in the refrigerator.

When ready to eat, reheat the stew in a pot or the microwave.

PER SERVING	
Calories	570
Protein	46 g
Fat	19 g
Carbohydrates	57 g
Fibre	5 g
Iron	4 mg
Calcium	143 mg
Sodium	835 mg

5•15 Tip

How to peel a squash

Tired of struggling with tough squash peels? Don't give up! Softening squash in the microwave for 2 to 3 minutes on high makes the job much easier! You can then place it on a cutting board, peel it with a vegetable peeler, slice it in half and remove the seeds with a spoon. A simple but effective tip!

Red curry paste
30 ml (2 tbsp)

①

Coconut milk
1 can (398 ml)

②

4 Italian tomatoes
cut into quarters

③

Dry lentils
pink or red
180 ml (¾ cup)

④

Chickpeas
rinsed and drained
1 can (540 ml)

⑤

Tomato, Lentil and Chickpea Hearty Soup

Prep time: **15 minutes** • Cook time: **27 minutes** • Serves: **4**

Preparation

Heat a little olive oil in a pot over medium heat. Cook the onion, garlic and ginger, if desired, for 1 minute.

Add the curry paste and cook for 30 seconds, until fragrant.

Add the coconut milk, tomatoes, lentils, stock and half of the chickpeas. Stir. Bring to a boil, and simmer for 25 to 30 minutes over medium-low heat.

Place the lentil preparation in the blender, mix for 1 minute until smooth and liquid.

Pour the soup into airtight containers. Then place the remaining chickpeas in the containers. Let the soup cool slightly on the counter, then refrigerate to cool completely.

Place the containers in the freezer.

The night before your meal, let the soup thaw out in the refrigerator.

When ready to eat, reheat the soup in a pot or the microwave.

PER SERVING	
Calories	503
Protein	21 g
Fat	22 g
Carbohydrates	59 g
Fibre	11 g
Iron	7 mg
Calcium	99 mg
Sodium	924 mg

Side Dish Idea

Tomato and Thai chili pepper garnish

In a bowl, mix 10 grape tomatoes, cut into quarters, with 30 ml (2 tbsp) chopped cilantro, 30 ml (2 tbsp) sesame oil (not toasted) and 1 Thai chili pepper, chopped.

ALSO NEEDED:
➤ **1 onion**
chopped

➤ **Vegetable stock**
500 ml (2 cups)

OPTIONAL:
➤ **Garlic**
2 cloves, minced

➤ **Ginger**
minced
15 ml (1 tbsp)

Beef ①
cubes for stew
750 g (1 ⅔ lb)

Garlic ②
minced
15 ml (1 tbsp)

Italian seasoning ③
15 ml (1 tbsp)

Diced tomatoes ④
1 can (796 ml)

Tomato juice ⑤
250 ml (1 cup)

ALSO NEEDED:
➤ **1 onion**
chopped
➤ **Flour**
30 ml (2 tbsp)

Italian-style Beef

Prep time: **15 minutes** • Cook time: **1 hour 30 minutes** • Serves: **4**

Preparation

Heat a little canola oil in a pot over medium heat. Brown a few beef cubes at a time for 2 to 3 minutes on each side.

Add the garlic and onion. Cook for 1 to 2 minutes.

Sprinkle with flour and cook for 1 minute, stirring.

Add the Italian seasoning, diced tomatoes and tomato juice. Bring to a boil. Cover and simmer for 1 hour and 30 minutes to 2 hours over low heat.

Put the preparation in airtight containers. Let it cool slightly on the counter, then refrigerate to cool completely. Place the containers in the freezer.

The night before your meal, let the containers thaw out in the refrigerator.

When ready to eat, reheat the preparation in a frying pan or the microwave.

PER SERVING	
Calories	427
Protein	44 g
Fat	18 g
Carbohydrates	20 g
Fibre	2 g
Iron	6 mg
Calcium	112 mg
Sodium	659 mg

Side Dish Idea

Garlic mashed potatoes

Place 6 unpeeled potatoes and 2 peeled whole garlic cloves in a pot. Cover with cold, salted water. Bring to a boil and cook for 15 to 20 minutes, until tender. Drain, then mash into a puree. Add 125 ml (½ cup) sour cream, 15 ml (1 tbsp) whole-grain mustard and 30 ml (2 tbsp) chopped chives. Season with salt and pepper.

Pork ①
cubes for stew
1 kg (about 2 ¼ lb)

Red wine ②
250 ml (1 cup)

Jellied cranberry sauce ③
250 ml (1 cup)

Shallots ④
chopped
60 ml (¼ cup)

Cranberries ⑤
fresh or dried
125 ml (½ cup)

ALSO NEEDED:
➤ **Flour**
30 ml (2 tbsp)
➤ **Brown sugar**
15 ml (1 tbsp)

OPTIONAL:
➤ **Rosemary**
chopped
5 ml (1 tsp)

Pork and Cranberry Stew

Prep time: **15 minutes** • Cook time on low: **7 hours** • Serves: **6**

Preparation

In a bowl, place the pork cubes and flour. Stir until the pork is fully coated with flour. Shake to remove excess flour.

Heat a little canola oil in a frying pan over medium-high heat. Brown the pork cubes on all sides. Place them in the slow cooker. Remove the cooking oil from the frying pan.

Add the red wine, cranberry sauce, brown sugar, and rosemary, if desired, to the frying pan. Bring to a boil, stirring occasionally. Pour into the slow cooker.

Add the shallots and cranberries to the slow cooker. Season with salt, and stir.

Cover and cook on low for 7 to 8 hours or on high for 4 to 6 hours.

Divide the stew into airtight containers. Let it cool slightly on the counter, then refrigerate to cool completely.

Place the containers in the freezer.

The night before your meal, let the stew thaw out in the refrigerator.

When ready to eat, reheat the stew.

PER SERVING	
Calories	402
Protein	36 g
Fat	12 g
Carbohydrates	27 g
Fibre	1 g
Iron	2 mg
Calcium	37 mg
Sodium	97 mg

Healthy Choice

Cranberries: Anytime, anywhere!

Cranberries are rich in antioxidants and can be enjoyed in many different ways. They're so much more than just the sidekick to your Thanksgiving turkey! Dried, frozen, jellied or fresh, these berries are packed with vitamins and can be savoured all year long in salads, yogurts and muffins, not to mention slow-cooked pork and chicken dishes!

Shallots ①
chopped
60 ml (¼ cup)

Mushrooms ②
sliced
1 container (227 g)

White wine ③
80 ml (⅓ cup)

2% milk ④
250 ml (1 cup)

Sole ⑤
8 fillets

OPTIONAL:
➤ **Parsley**
chopped
30 ml (2 tbsp)

Creamy Mushroom Sole

Prep time: **15 minutes** • Cook time: **15 minutes** • Serves: **4**

Preparation

Melt a little butter in a frying pan over medium heat. Cook the shallots and mushrooms for 2 to 3 minutes.

Add the wine and cook for 2 to 3 minutes.

Add the milk and bring to a boil.

Place the sole fillets in the frying pan. Season with salt and pepper. Cover and simmer for 15 to 18 minutes over medium-low heat.

Remove from heat. Let cool slightly on the counter, then refrigerate to cool completely.

Divide the fillets and sauce into airtight containers. Place the containers in the freezer.

The night before your meal, let the containers thaw out in the refrigerator.

When ready to eat, reheat the fillets and sauce in a frying pan or the microwave.

Sprinkle with parsley before serving, if desired.

PER SERVING	
Calories	303
Protein	42 g
Fat	10 g
Carbohydrates	7 g
Fibre	1 g
Iron	1 mg
Calcium	125 mg
Sodium	199 mg

Side Dish Idea

Bean, tomato and mozzarella salad

In a pot of boiling, salted water, blanch 250 g (about ½ lb) green and yellow beans for 3 to 5 minutes, until tender. Rinse under very cold water and drain. Cut the beans into pieces. In a salad bowl, mix 60 ml (¼ cup) olive oil, 15 ml (1 tbsp) balsamic vinegar and 15 ml (1 tbsp) honey. Add 12 cherry tomatoes, sliced in half, 1 package of fresh mozzarella (250 g), cut into small cubes, and the beans. Season with salt and pepper, and stir well.

Beef 1
cubes for stew
675 g (about 1 ½ lb)

White wine 2
250 ml (1 cup)

Chili sauce 3
60 ml (¼ cup)

Red wine vinegar 4
45 ml (3 tbsp)

Brown sugar 5
30 ml (2 tbsp)

ALSO NEEDED:
➤ **1 onion**
  chopped
➤ **Beef stock**
125 ml (½ cup)

OPTIONAL:
➤ **Garlic**
  diced
  15 ml (1 tbsp)
➤ **1 jalapeno**
  deseeded and finely
  chopped

Texan Beef Stew

Prep time: **15 minutes** • Cooking time on low: **8 hours** • Serves: **4**

Preparation

Heat a little canola oil in a frying pan over medium heat. Brown the beef cubes on all sides.

Add the onion and cook for 1 minute, stirring.

Place the beef and onion in the slow cooker.

In a bowl, mix the white wine, chili sauce, red wine vinegar, brown sugar and beef stock. Mix in the garlic and jalapeno, if desired. Pour the preparation into the slow cooker.

Cover and cook on low for 8 to 10 hours.

Put the stew in airtight containers. Let it cool slightly on the counter, then refrigerate to cool completely.

Place the containers in the freezer.

The night before your meal, let the stew thaw out in the refrigerator.

When ready to eat, reheat the stew in a pot or the microwave.

Chef's Secret

Stews are much better reheated!

Ask any chef—stews taste even better when they've been reheated. This Texas-style delicacy is no exception! The rest time between preparing and actually eating the stew lets the meat get tender and absorb the taste of the sauce, spices and vegetables mixed in with it. Get ahead without compromising flavour by preparing a delectable stew, and freezing it!

PER SERVING	
Calories	420
Protein	38 g
Fat	17 g
Carbohydrates	13 g
Fibre	2 g
Iron	4 mg
Calcium	39 mg
Sodium	449 mg

2 carrots ①
sliced into rounds

Celery ②
2 stalks, chopped

Chicken stock ③
low sodium
2 litres (8 cups)

Long grain white rice ④
125 ml (½ cup)

Chicken ⑤
4 breasts
cooked and shredded

OPTIONAL:
➤ **Thyme**
chopped
15 ml (1 tbsp)

ALSO NEEDED:
➤ **2 onions**
chopped

➤ **Parsley**
chopped
30 ml (2 tbsp)

Chicken and Rice Soup

Prep time: **15 minutes** • Cook time: **50 minutes** • Serves: **8**

Preparation

Heat a little oil and butter in a pot over medium heat. Brown the onions for 1 to 2 minutes.

Add the carrots, celery, stock and thyme, if desired. Cover and simmer over low heat for 30 minutes.

Add the rice and cook for another 18 to 20 minutes over low heat, until the rice is cooked.

Add the chicken, and parsley, if desired. Heat for 1 to 2 minutes.

Remove the pot from the heat. Let it cool slightly on the counter, then refrigerate to cool completely.

Pour the soup into airtight containers. Place the containers in the freezer.

The night before your meal, let the soup thaw out in the refrigerator.

When ready to eat, reheat the soup in a pot or the microwave.

PER SERVING	
Calories	432
Protein	28 g
Fat	29 g
Carbohydrates	15 g
Fibre	1 g
Iron	2 mg
Calcium	32 mg
Sodium	746 mg

Chef's Secret

How to make chicken stock at home

It goes without saying that store-bought chicken stock is more convenient for whipping up a quick meal, but nothing compares to the old-fashioned stuff—homemade chicken stock! The next time you have a leftover chicken carcass on your hands, boil it in a pot over low heat for an hour without a lid and with light seasoning (carrots, celery, onions, garlic, thyme and a bay leaf), then strain the stock and freeze the liquid. Now you'll always have chicken stock around when you need it!

Medium ground beef ①
300 g (⅔ lb)

Pizza sauce ②
180 ml (¾ cup)

Pizza dough ③
600 g (1 ⅓ lb)

1 green bell pepper ④
diced

Shredded four cheese blend ⑤
375 ml (1 ½ cups)

ALSO NEEDED:

➤ **Egg**
1 yolk beaten with
a little water

Beef Pizza Pockets

Prep time:: **15 minutes** • Cook time: **33 minutes** • Serves: **4**

Preparation

Preheat the oven to 205°C (400°F).

Heat a little olive oil in a frying pan over medium heat. Cook the ground beef for 4 to 5 minutes, breaking up the meat with a wooden spoon, until it is no longer pink.

Add the pizza sauce, and stir. Cook for 4 minutes. Remove the pan from the heat and let it cool on the counter.

Divide the pizza dough into four parts. On a floured surface, roll out each part into a circle, 20 cm (8 in) in diameter.

Top half of each circle with the beef preparation, bell pepper and shredded cheese, leaving a 2 cm (¾ in) perimeter free for the crust.

Brush the edges of the circles with the egg yolk.

Fold the dough over the toppings and seal the edges with a fork. Brush the top of the pizza pockets with the remaining egg yolk.

Place the pizzas on a baking sheet lined with parchment paper. Bake for 25 to 30 minutes.

Remove the baking sheet from the oven. Let it cool slightly on the counter, then refrigerate to cool completely.

Place the pizzas in a large freezer bag. Remove the air from the bag and seal it. Place the bag in the freezer.

The night before your meal, let the pizza pockets thaw out in the refrigerator.

When ready to eat, reheat the pizza pockets in the oven or microwave.

PER SERVING	
Calories	721
Protein	38 g
Fat	29 g
Carbohydrates	74 g
Fibres	4 g
Iron	7 mg
Calcium	301 mg
Sodium	865 mg

Mix It Up

Opt for ground veal

Beef and veal can be distinguished from one another by their colour and taste: beef is a red meat with a bolder flavour, while veal is a lean white meat with a slightly less pronounced flavour. Perhaps more importantly, they each offer different health benefits. In equal quantities of calories and protein, veal is lower in fat, saturated fatty acids and cholesterol than beef. On the other hand, beef contains slightly more minerals than veal. Both of these meats have significant nutritional value—the secret is to alternate them!

32 butter crackers
crushed
①

Crab meat
450 g (1 lb)
fully drained
②

Panko breadcrumbs
125 ml (½ cup)
③

Mayonnaise
60 ml (¼ cup)
④

Lemon zest
15 ml (1 tbsp)
⑤

ALSO NEEDED:
➢ **2% milk**
60 ml (¼ cup)
➢ **1 egg**
beaten

OPTIONAL:
➢ **Dill**
chopped
30 ml (2 tbsp)
➢ **Chives**
chopped
45 ml (3 tbsp)

Crab Cakes

Prep time: **15 minutes** • Rest time: **5 minutes** • Cook time: **20 minutes** • Serves: **4 (8 crab cakes)**

Preparation

Preheat the oven to 205°C (400°F).

In a bowl, mix the crackers and milk. Let sit for 5 minutes.

Add the crab, breadcrumbs, mayonnaise, zest and beaten egg. Add the dill and chives, if desired. Season with salt and pepper, and stir until even.

Form 8 balls, using about 80 ml (⅓ cup) of the preparation for each.

Butter 8 cups of a muffin tin, and place one crab ball into each. Lightly press the balls into the muffin tin cups.

Bake for 20 to 25 minutes. Remove the muffin tin from the oven. Let it cool slightly on the counter, then refrigerate to cool completely.

Place the crab cakes in a large freezer bag. Remove the air from the bag and seal it. Place the bag in the freezer.

The night before your meal, let the crab cakes thaw out in the refrigerator.

When ready to eat, reheat the crab cakes in the oven or microwave.

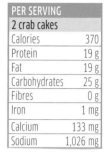

PER SERVING	
2 crab cakes	
Calories	370
Protein	19 g
Fat	19 g
Carbohydrates	25 g
Fibres	0 g
Iron	1 mg
Calcium	133 mg
Sodium	1,026 mg

Side Dish Idea

Herbed tartar sauce

Mix 125 ml (½ cup) mayonnaise, 45 ml (3 tbsp) plain Greek yogurt, 30 ml (2 tbsp) chopped pickles, 15 ml (1 tbsp) chopped capers, 30 ml (2 tbsp) chopped chives, 30 ml (2 tbsp) chopped parsley and 30 ml (2 tbsp) chopped dill. Season with salt and pepper.

**Farfalles
(bow tie pasta)**
750 ml (3 cups)

Cream cheese
1 container (250 g)

Parmesan
grated
250 ml (1 cup)

Chicken
cooked and diced
500 ml (2 cups)

Sun-dried tomatoes
minced
180 ml (¾ cup)

ALSO NEEDED:
➤ **2% milk**
500 ml (2 cups)

➤ **Garlic**
minced
15 ml (1 tbsp)

Creamy Chicken Pasta

Prep time: **15 minutes** • Cook time: **25 minutes** • Serves: **4**

Preparation

In a pot of boiling, salted water, cook the pasta *al dente*. Drain.

In the same pot, add the cream cheese, parmesan, milk and garlic. Season with salt and pepper. Bring to a boil, stirring.

Remove from heat. Use an immersion blender to mix until smooth.

Add the cooked chicken, sun-dried tomatoes and pasta. Stir. Transfer to a baking dish. Let it cool slightly on the counter, then refrigerate to cool completely.

Cover the dish in plastic wrap and aluminum foil. Place the dish in the freezer.

The night before your meal, let the dish thaw out in the refrigerator.

When ready to cook, preheat the oven to 205°C (400°F).

Remove the aluminum foil and plastic wrap from the dish. Bake for 25 to 30 minutes.

PER SERVING	
Calories	731
Protein	49 g
Fat	37 g
Carbohydrates	52 g
Fibres	3 g
Iron	3 mg
Calcium	565 mg
Sodium	821 mg

Chef's Secret

Which sun-dried tomatoes should I buy?

For a quick meal, choose oil-packed sun-dried tomatoes. That way, you don't have to rehydrate them. Just add them to your pasta dishes, omelettes, sauces and gratins to give your meal a little Italian flair! You can also use the oil to flavour dressings and marinades. Keep in mind that once the jar is opened, sun-dried tomatoes keep for one month in the fridge.

Pizza dough 1
400 g (about 1 lb)

Basil pesto 2
80 ml (⅓ cup)

Cold water shrimp 3
300 g (⅔ lb)

Roasted red bell peppers 4
diced
160 ml (⅔ cup)

Mozzarella 5
shredded
250 ml (1 cup)

ALSO NEEDED:
➤ **Green onion**
chopped
30 ml (2 tbsp)

➤ **1 egg**

Shrimp and Pesto Stromboli

Prep time: **15 minutes** • Cook time: **15 minutes** • Serves: **4**

Preparation

Preheat the oven to 205°C (400°F).

Stretch out the pizza dough into a rectangle, 35 cm x 25 cm (14 in x 10 in). Brush the dough with pesto, leaving a 2 cm (¾ in) border along the short sides and a border about 6 cm (2 ½ in) on one of the long sides.

Top the dough with shrimp, roasted bell peppers and green onion. Cover with mozzarella.

In a small bowl, whisk the egg with about 15 ml (1 tbsp) water, and brush it over the edges of the dough.

Roll the stromboli, following the instructions given below.

Place the stromboli on a baking sheet lined with parchment paper. Bake for 15 to 18 minutes.

Remove from the oven. Let the stromboli cool slightly on the counter, then refrigerate to cool completely.

Place the stromboli in a large freezer bag. Remove the air from the bag and seal it. Place the bag flat in the freezer.

The night before your meal, let the stromboli thaw out in the refrigerator.

When ready to eat, reheat the stromboli in the oven or microwave. Cut it into slices.

PER SERVING	
Calories	527
Protein	29 g
Fat	24 g
Carbohydrates	47 g
Fibres	0 g
Iron	4 mg
Calcium	202 mg
Sodium	1,081 mg

Chef's Secret

How to roll a stromboli

Fold the long edge of the dough over to cover a third of the filling

Fold the dough over itself a second time to form a roll. Press the dough along the edges to seal it. Brush the top of the stromboli with the beaten egg and water. Use a small knife to cut a couple of vents in the top of the dough to let steam escape.

Blend of three ground meats
(beef, pork and veal)
900 g (2 lb)

Diced tomatoes with spices
1 can (796 ml)

Condensed tomato soup
1 can (284 ml)

Parboiled long grain white rice
180 ml (¾ cup)

Savoy cabbage
chopped
2.5 litres (10 cups)

ALSO NEEDED:
➤ **1 onion**
diced
➤ **Parsley**
chopped
60 ml (¼ cup)

OPTIONAL:
➤ **Garlic**
minced
15 ml (1 tbsp)

Unstuffed Cabbage Rolls

Prep time: **15 minutes** • Cook time: **2 hours** • Serves: **6**

Preparation

In a bowl, mix the ground meats, onion, and garlic, if desired. Season with salt and pepper.

In another bowl, mix the diced tomatoes, tomato soup, parsley and 250 ml (1 cup) water.

Place half of the meat preparation in a lightly greased 33 cm x 23 cm (13 in x 9 in) baking dish. Sprinkle with half of the rice, tomato preparation and cabbage. Even out the surface by lightly pressing on the preparation. Repeat these steps once again.

Cover the baking dish with plastic wrap and then aluminum foil. Place the baking dish in the freezer.

The night before your meal, let the dish thaw out in the refrigerator.

When ready to cook, preheat the oven to 180°C (350°F).

Remove the aluminum foil and the plastic wrap from the baking dish. Put the aluminum foil back over the baking dish. Bake for 1 hour and 30 minutes to 2 hours.

Remove the aluminum foil from the baking dish and cook for another 30 minutes. Let sit for 5 to 10 minutes before serving.

PER SERVING	
Calories	559
Protein	34 g
Fat	26 g
Carbohydrates	48 g
Fibres	8 g
Iron	4 mg
Calcium	142 mg
Sodium	787 mg

Learn More

Savoy cabbage

Savoy cabbage is tender and sweet, and is milder than green cabbage. Look for cabbage heads that are solid green in colour and slightly cone-shaped. The leaves should also be firm. Savoy cabbage keeps for about a week in refrigerator crisper drawers.

Sole
fillets
450 g (1 lb)
cut into cubes

1

Plain bread crumbs
80 ml (⅓ cup)

2

Light mayonnaise
15 ml (1 tbsp)

3

Dijon mustard
15 ml (1 tbsp)

4

Lemon juice
15 ml (1 tbsp)

5

ALSO NEEDED:
➤ **Parsley**
chopped
60 ml (¼ cup)
➤ **1 egg**

OPTIONAL:
➤ **2 green onions**
chopped

Sole Croquettes

Prep time: **15 minutes** • Refrigerating time: **30 minutes** • Cook time: **8 minutes** • Serves: **4**

Preparation

Place the sole, bread crumbs, mayonnaise, mustard, lemon juice, parsley, egg, and green onion, if desired, in the food processer. Season with salt and pepper. Blend until coarsely chopped. Refrigerate for 30 minutes.

Form 8 croquettes, using about 80 ml (⅓ cup) of preparation for each.

Heat a little olive oil in a frying pan over medium heat. Cook the croquettes for 4 to 5 minutes on each side.

Remove from heat, let cool slightly on the counter, then refrigerate to cool completely.

Place the croquettes in a large freezer bag. Remove the air from the bag and seal it. Place the bag in the freezer.

The night before your meal, let the croquettes thaw out in the refrigerator.

When ready to eat, reheat the croquettes in the oven for 10 to 12 minutes at 205°C (400°F).

PER SERVING	
Calories	207
Protein	24 g
Fat	8 g
Carbohydrates	8 g
Fibres	1 g
Iron	1 mg
Calcium	55 mg
Sodium	254 mg

Side Dish Idea

Lemon and mint yogurt sauce

In a bowl, mix 125 ml (½ cup) plain Greek yogurt, 15 ml (1 tbsp) chopped mint, 15 ml (1 tbsp) lemon zest and 5 ml (1 tsp) minced garlic. Season with salt and pepper.

Fettuccine ❶
260 g (about ½ lb)

Light cream cheese ❷
1 container (250 g)

Parmesan ❸
grated
80 ml (⅓ cup)

Parsley ❹
chopped
30 ml (2 tbsp)

Thyme ❺
leaves from 1 sprig

ALSO NEEDED:
➤ **Garlic**
1 clove, minced

Light Fettuccine Alfredo

Prep time: **15 minutes** • Cook time: **12 minutes** • Serves: **4**

Preparation

In a pot of boiling, salted water, cook the fettuccine al dente. Drain, keeping 125 ml (½ cup) cooking water.

In the same pot, melt the cream cheese with 60 ml (¼ cup) cooking water over low heat, stirring.

Add the parmesan, parsley, thyme and garlic. Stir.

Put the pasta back in the pot and mix well. Season generously with pepper. If the preparation seems too dry, add a little more cooking water.

Place the pasta in airtight containers. Let them cool slightly on the counter, then refrigerate to cool completely.

Place the containers in the freezer.

The night before your meal, let the pasta thaw out in the refrigerator.

When ready to eat, reheat the pasta in a pot or the microwave.

PER SERVING	
Calories	394
Protein	16 g
Fat	13 g
Carbohydrates	54 g
Fibres	3 g
Iron	2 mg
Calcium	223 mg
Sodium	438 mg

Learn More

Who is the creator behind Alfredo pasta?

The story goes that an Italian cook named Alfredo Di Lelio developed this sauce to increase his wife's appetite during her pregnancy. He gave his name to the famous fettuccine dish and later served it in the restaurant he opened in Rome in 1914. More than a hundred years later, the recipe calls for the same ingredients: butter, cream and parmesan. We've modified our version to make it slightly less rich, but it's just as delicious!

1 leek ①
chopped

1 carrot ②
cut into thin
julienne strips

Frozen puff pastry ③
thawed
2 packages
(400 g each)

Salmon ④
8 fillets
150 g (⅓ lb) each
skin removed

Egg ⑤
1 yolk beaten
with a little water

Salmon Wellington

Prep time: **15 minutes** • Cook time: **30 minutes** • Serves: **8**

Preparation

Heat a little olive oil in a frying pan over medium heat. Cook the leek and carrot for 2 to 3 minutes. Remove the pan from the heat and let it cool on the counter.

Roll out the dough from one package on a lightly floured surface and cut it into 8 rectangles, 15.5 cm x 7.5 cm (6 in x 3 in) each. Place the rectangles on a baking sheet lined with parchment paper. Roll out the dough from the other package and cut it into 8 rectangles, 18 cm x 10 cm (7 in x 4 in) each. Place a salmon fillet at the centre of each of the smaller dough rectangles. Top the fillets with the vegetable preparation.

Brush the edges of the dough with the egg yolk. Cover with the remaining dough and seal the edges with a fork.

Place the Wellingtons in the freezer for 2 to 3 hours.

Wrap each Wellington in a layer of aluminum foil. Place them in freezer bags. Remove the air from the bags and seal them. Place the bags in the freezer.

The night before your meal, let the bags thaw out in the refrigerator.

When ready to cook, preheat the oven to 190°C (375°F).

Remove the aluminum foil from the Wellingtons. Place the frozen Wellingtons on a baking sheet lined with parchment paper.

Brush the dough with a little egg yolk.

Cook the Wellingtons in the oven for 30 minutes, until the crust is golden-brown.

PER SERVING	
Calories	893
Protein	38 g
Fat	61 g
Carbohydrates	47 g
Fibres	2 g
Iron	3 mg
Calcium	33 mg
Sodium	341 mg

Side Dish Idea

Creamy white wine and parmesan sauce

In a pot, bring 125 ml (½ cup) white wine with 60 ml (¼ cup) chopped shallots to a boil over medium heat. Simmer, reducing until no liquid remains in the pot. Pour 375 ml (1½ cups) cooking cream (15%) and simmer for 5 to 6 minutes over low heat. Add 30 ml (2 tbsp) chopped chives, 30 ml (2 tbsp) chopped dill and 60 ml (¼ cup) grated parmesan. Season with salt and pepper.

Black beans
rinsed and drained
1 can (540 ml)

1

Corn kernels
frozen
250 ml (1 cup)

2

Salsa
125 ml (½ cup)

3

Tortillas
8 medium-sized

4

Tex-Mex shredded cheese
500 ml (2 cups)

5

Vegetarian Burritos

Prep time: **15 minutes** • Cook time: **25 minutes** • Serves: **4**

Preparation

In a bowl, mix the beans, corn and salsa. Season with salt and pepper.

Distribute the bean preparation and cheese into the centre of each tortilla. Roll up the tortillas tightly and place them on a baking sheet lined with parchment paper. Place the baking sheet in the freezer for 3 hours.

Place the burritos in freezer bags. Remove the air from the bags and seal. Place the bags in the freezer.

The night before your meal, let the burritos thaw out in the refrigerator.

When ready to cook, preheat the oven to 205°C (400°F).

Place the burritos on a baking sheet lined with a layer of parchment paper. Bake for 25 to 30 minutes.

PER SERVING	
Calories	514
Protein	26 g
Fat	18 g
Carbohydrates	62 g
Fibres	9 g
Iron	3 mg
Calcium	72 mg
Sodium	1,037 mg

Homemade Version

Salsa

Heat 30 ml (2 tbsp) olive oil in a pot. Cook 2 diced onions and 15 ml (1 tbsp) minced garlic for 2 to 3 minutes. Add 4 diced bell peppers of various colours, 8 to 10 diced tomatoes, 1 deseeded and chopped jalapeno, 60 ml (¼ cup) tomato paste, 60 ml (¼ cup) red wine vinegar and 45 ml (3 tbsp) sugar. Bring to a boil and simmer for 20 to 25 minutes over low heat. Add 45 ml (3 tbsp) chopped cilantro and stir. Cook for 5 minutes.

Tuna and Vegetable Casserole

Prep time: **15 minutes** • Cook time: **25 minutes** • Serves: **6**

6 large potatoes ①
Russet, Idaho
or Yukon Gold

Flour ②
125 ml (½ cup)

2% milk ③
625 ml (2 ½ cups)

Tuna ④
drained
2 cans (170 g each)

Frozen mixed vegetables ⑤
thawed
750 ml (3 cups)

ALSO NEEDED:
➤ **Butter**
80 ml (⅓ cup)
➤ **1 onion**
diced

OPTIONAL:
➤ **Parsley**
45 ml (3 tbsp)
chopped

Preparation

Peel and cut the potatoes into cubes. Place the potatoes in a pot and cover with cold water. Bring to a boil and cook for 20 minutes over medium heat.

While the potatoes are cooking, melt the butter in another pot. Brown the onion for 2 to 3 minutes.

Sprinkle with flour and cook for 1 minute, stirring. Pour in the milk and bring to a boil, whisking. Season with salt and pepper.

Add the tuna, mixed vegetable and parsley, if desired, to the sauce.

Divide the preparation into small aluminum baking dishes, 14.5 cm x 12 cm (5 ¾ in x 4 ¾ in) each, or in a rectangular baking dish, 33 cm x 23 cm (13 in x 9 in).

Drain the potatoes and mash them into a puree. Spread the puree onto the prepared tuna. Let it cool slightly on the counter, then refrigerate to cool completely.

Cover the baking dishes with plastic wrap and then aluminum foil. Place them in the freezer.

The night before your meal, let the casserole thaw out in the refrigerator.

When ready to cook, preheat the oven to 180°C (350°F).

Remove the aluminum foil and plastic wrap from the baking dishes. Bake for 25 to 30 minutes.

5•15 Tip

We're all for canned tuna!

There's nothing more convenient than a ready-made protein when you need a quick meal—especially when it's easy on the budget! Having canned tuna on hand is a great way to avoid being caught off guard with nothing to eat. Keep your pantry stocked and you'll always be able to prepare a delicious, balanced meal in no time at all. And remember to always fully drain tuna before using it!

PER SERVING	
Calories	561
Protein	30 g
Fat	14 g
Carbohydrates	93 g
Fibres	9 g
Iron	5 mg
Calcium	219 mg
Sodium	203 mg

Pork and Ratatouille Noodles

Prep time: **15 minutes** • Cook time: **14 minutes** • Serves: **4**

Preparation

Heat a little olive oil in a pot over medium heat. Brown the pork tenderloins on all surfaces for 2 to 3 minutes.

Add the diced tomatoes and bring to a boil.

Add the zucchinis, eggplant, garlic, onion and carrots, if desired. Season with salt and pepper. Cover and simmer for 12 to 15 minutes over medium heat.

Remove the pot from the heat. Let it cool slightly on the counter, then refrigerate to cool completely.

Place the pork and ratatouille in airtight containers. Place the containers in the freezer.

The night before your meal, let the containers thaw out in the refrigerator.

When ready to eat, cook the noodles according to the instructions on the packaging. Drain.

Reheat the pork and ratatouille in a frying pan or the microwave. Serve with the noodles.

PER SERVING	
Calories	674
Protein	56 g
Fat	12 g
Carbohydrates	87 g
Fibre	9 g
Iron	7 mg
Calcium	158 mg
Sodium	452 mg

Learn More

Ratatouille

Ratatouille is a stew made of seasoned vegetables that is typical of France's Provence region. Its name comes from the French verb *touiller*, which means "to stir." It is usually made of eggplants, onions, zucchinis, bell peppers, tomatoes and garlic. Although it is often served alongside fish or chicken, it also pairs well with pork and can even be prepared as the main dish with a side of rice. Enjoy hot or cold—either way is delicious!

Pork ①
2 tenderloins
350 g (around ¾ lb) each

Diced tomatoes ②
1 can (796 ml)

2 zucchinis ③
cut into cubes

1 small eggplant ④
cut into cubes

Egg noodles ⑤
1 package (340 g)

ALSO NEEDED:
➤ **Garlic**
minced
15 ml (1 tbsp)

➤ **1 onion**
chopped

OPTIONAL:
➤ **2 carrots**
diced

Pancetta or bacon 1
pre-cooked and diced
80 g (about 2¾ oz)

Baby spinach 2
1 litre (4 cups)

Salmon 3
1 fillet
300 g (⅔ lb)
skin removed
and diced

1 pie crust 4

Cooking cream (15%) 5
80 ml (⅓ cup)

ALSO NEEDED:
➤ **3 eggs**

OPTIONAL:
➤ **Dill**
60 ml (¼ cup)
chopped

Salmon and Pancetta Quiche

Prep time: **15 minutes** • Cook time: **35 minutes** • Serves: **4**

Preparation

Preheat the oven to 190°C (375°F).

Heat a little olive oil in a frying pan over medium heat. Cook the pancetta and baby spinach for 1 to 2 minutes. Remove the pan from the heat and let it cool on the counter.

Place the pancetta preparation and diced salmon into the pie crust.

In a bowl, whisk the eggs, cream, and dill, if desired. Season with salt and pepper. Pour the mix into the pie crust.

Bake for 35 to 40 minutes.

Remove the pie crust from the oven. Let it cool slightly on the counter, then refrigerate to cool completely.

Wrap the quiche in plastic wrap and then aluminum foil. Place the quiche in the freezer.

The night before your meal, let the quiche thaw out in the refrigerator.

When ready to eat, remove the aluminum foil and plastic wrap. Reheat the quiche in the oven or microwave.

5•15 Tip

Opt for pre-cooked, pre-cut pancetta

To liven up a pasta dish, bring out the taste of an omelette or add a little extra flavour to a salad, Italian charcuteries can work miracles. To save time in the kitchen, opt for pancetta that is already cooked and diced—adding it to your everyday recipes is as easy as pie!

PER SERVING	
Calories	547
Protein	29 g
Fat	39 g
Carbohydrates	20 g
Fibre	3 g
Iron	2 mg
Calcium	75 mg
Sodium	553 mg

Condensed cream of chicken soup
1 can (284 ml)

1

Dijon mustard
5 ml (1 tsp)

2

Frozen mixed vegetables
375 ml (1 ½ cups)

3

Chicken
cooked and diced
500 ml (2 cups)

4

Pie dough
300 g (⅔ lb)

5

ALSO NEEDED:

➤ **2% milk**
125 ml (½ cup)

➤ **Egg**
1 yolk, beaten

Quick Chicken Pot Pie

Prep time: **15 minutes** • Cook time: **20 minutes** • Serves: 4

Preparation

Preheat the oven to 205°C (400°F).

In a pot, mix the cream of chicken, Dijon mustard and milk. Heat over medium heat for 5 minutes.

Add the mixed vegetables and cooked chicken. Bring to a boil and simmer over low heat for 5 minutes.

Divide the preparation into four small baking dishes or ramekins.

On a lightly floured surface, roll out the dough into 4 squares, slightly bigger than the size of the baking dishes.

Brush the edges of the baking dishes with the beaten egg yolk, and then place a dough square on each one. Press the dough against the edges of the baking dishes to seal it.

Bake for 10 minutes. Remove the baking dishes from the oven. Let them cool slightly on the counter, then refrigerate to cool completely.

Cover the baking dishes with plastic wrap and then aluminum foil. Place them in the freezer.

The night before your meal, let the chicken pot pies thaw out in the refrigerator.

When ready to eat, remove the aluminum foil and plastic wrap from the baking dishes. Reheat the pies in the oven or microwave.

5•15 Tip

Make extra!

This classic savoury pie keeps well in the freezer, so it's a perfect quick fix for weeknight appetites. Since it can be frozen for up to 3 months, feel free to cook several at one time: it's a super convenient and tasty solution for dinner!

PER SERVING	
Calories	537
Protein	32 g
Fat	25 g
Carbohydrates	51 g
Fibre	4 g
Iron	2 mg
Calcium	88 mg
Sodium	849 mg

Recipe by Rebecca Bouchard

Chicken ①
skinless breasts
450 g (1 lb)

Plain bread crumbs ②
60 ml (¼ cup)

Cilantro ③
chopped
30 ml (2 tbsp)

Soy sauce ④
15 ml (1 tbsp)

Ginger ⑤
minced
15 ml (1 tbsp)

ALSO NEEDED:
➤ **Garlic**
minced
5 ml (1 tsp)

➤ **1 egg**
beaten

OPTIONAL:
➤ **Lime zest**
10 ml (2 tsp)

Mini Chicken Cilantro Croquettes

Prep time: **15 minutes** • Cook time: **12 minutes** • Serves: **4 (12 mini croquettes)**

Preparation

Cut the chicken breasts into pieces. Place the pieces in the food processor and coarsely chop.

Transfer the chicken to a large bowl. Add the rest of the ingredients and mix well.

Form 12 thin croquettes, using about 45 ml (3 tbsp) of preparation for each one.

Heat a little sesame oil (not toasted) or canola oil in a large pan over medium heat. Cook half the croquettes for 3 to 4 minutes on each side, until they are no longer pink in the centre. Set aside on a plate and repeat with the rest of the croquettes.

Let the croquettes cool slightly on the counter, then refrigerate to cool completely.

Place the croquettes in a large freezer bag. Remove the air from the bag and seal it. Place the bag in the freezer.

The night before your meal, let the croquettes thaw out in the refrigerator.

When ready to eat, reheat the croquettes in the oven or microwave.

PER SERVING	
3 mini croquettes	
Calories	217
Protein	28 g
Fat	8 g
Carbohydrates	6 g
Fibre	1 g
Iron	1 mg
Calcium	29 mg
Sodium	340 mg

Side Dish Idea

Yogurt, lime and chive sauce

Mix 125 ml (½ cup) plain Greek yogurt with 30 ml (2 tbsp) chopped chives, 15 ml (1 tbsp) lime juice, 10 ml (2 tsp) lime zest and 5 ml (1 tsp) paprika. Season with salt and pepper.

1 onion
chopped ①

Italian diced tomatoes
1 can (796 ml) ②

Tomato paste
30 ml (2 tbsp) ③

Basil ④
chopped
60 ml (¼ cup)

Spaghetti noodles ⑤
360 g (about ¾ lb)

ALSO NEEDED:
➤ **Sugar**
15 ml (1 tbsp)

OPTIONAL:
➤ **Garlic**
minced
15 ml (1 tbsp)

Marinara Sauce Spaghetti

Prep time: **15 minutes** • Cook time: **30 minutes** • Serves: **4**

Preparation

Heat a little olive oil in a pot over medium heat. Sear the onion and garlic, if desired, for 1 to 2 minutes.

Add the tomatoes, including the juice, tomato paste and sugar. Season with salt and pepper, and stir. Bring to a boil, and then cover and simmer for 25 minutes over low heat.

Add the basil and simmer for 5 minutes. For a sauce that's smooth throughout, blend into a puree with an immersion blender.

While the sauce is cooking, cook the pasta *al dente* in a pot of boiling, salted water. Drain.

Pour the sauce and the pasta into airtight containers. Let the containers cool slightly on the counter, then refrigerate to cool completely. Place the containers in the freezer.

The night before your meal, let the containers thaw out in the refrigerator.

When ready to eat, reheat the containers in the microwave.

PER SERVING	
Calories	490
Protein	15 g
Fat	9 g
Carbohydrates	90 g
Fibre	6 g
Iron	5 mg
Calcium	113 mg
Sodium	490 mg

Chef's Secret

Use fresh tomatoes

Marinara sauce is delicious on pasta, but it also pairs well with a host of other foods, such as veal cutlets, mussels and cheese sticks. To make it, you can use fresh Italian tomatoes instead of canned ones, but only when they're in season and fully ripe. Simply replace the can of tomatoes in this recipe with 450 g (1 lb) of Italian tomatoes.

Ground pork ①
200 g (about ½ lb)

Maple syrup ②
15 ml (1 tbsp)

Paprika ③
5 ml (1 tsp)

2 green onions ④
chopped

Pie dough ⑤
450 g (about 1 lb)

ALSO NEEDED:

➤ **Garlic**
minced
5 ml (1 tsp)

➤ **Egg**
1 yolk beaten
with a little water

Mini Maple Tourtieres

Prep time: **15 minutes** • Cook time: **20 minutes** • Serves: **4 (12 mini tourtieres)**

Preparation

Preheat the oven to 180°C (350°F).

In a bowl, mix the ground pork, maple syrup, paprika, green onions and garlic. Set aside in a cool place.

Roll the dough on a lightly floured surface. Use a cookie cutter or a glass to cut 12 circles, 6.5 cm (2 ½ in) in diameter each and 12 larger circles, 7.5 cm (3 in) in diameter each.

Place 15 ml (1 tbsp) of filling in the centre of each small circle. Brush the edges of the small circles with the egg yolk. Place the larger circles over the filling and seal the edges.

Cut four slits in the top of each mini tourtiere.

Place them on a baking sheet lined with parchment paper and brush the tops with the rest of the egg yolk.

Bake on the lower rack of the oven for 20 to 25 minutes, until the filling is hot and the pastry is golden.

Remove the tray from the oven and let the mini tourtieres cool slightly on the counter, then refrigerate to cool completely.

Place the mini tourtieres in a large freezer bag, remove the air from the bag and seal it. Place the bag in the freezer.

The night before the meal, let the bag thaw out in the refrigerator.

When ready to eat, reheat the mini tourtieres in the oven or the microwave.

PER SERVING	
3 mini tourtieres	
Calories	633
Protein	16 g
Fat	36 g
Carbohydrates	58 g
Fibre	2 g
Iron	2 mg
Calcium	42 mg
Sodium	405 mg

Chef's Secret

Wow your guests with miniature pastries!

This reinvented miniature take on tourtiere breathes new life into a traditional dish. Served in dainty small portions, these elegant pastries with a hint of maple are ideal for cocktail parties and add a touch of glamour to any event!

Pie dough 1
250 g (about ½ lb)

Bacon 2
8 slices
cooked and broken
up into bits

Gruyère cheese 3
shredded
375 ml (1 ½ cups)

4 eggs 4

Cooking cream (15%) 5
500 ml (2 cups)

OPTIONAL:
➤ **Nutmeg**
1.25 ml (¼ tsp)

Quiche Lorraine

Prep time: **15 minutes** • Cook time: **40 minutes** • Serves: **4**

Preparation

Preheat the oven to 180°C (350°F).

On a floured surface, roll out the dough into a 25 cm (10 in) circle. Place in a pie pan, 23 cm (9 in) in diameter.

Place the bacon pieces onto the bottom of the crust, alternating with the cheese.

In a bowl, whisk the eggs, cream and nutmeg, if desired. Season with salt and pepper. Pour into the crust.

Bake for 40 to 45 minutes, until the quiche is no longer liquid in the centre.

Remove the quiche from the oven. Let it cool slightly on the counter, then refrigerate to cool completely.

Cover the quiche with plastic wrap and then aluminum foil. Place the quiche in the freezer.

The night before your meal, let the quiche thaw out in the refrigerator.

When ready to eat, remove the aluminum foil and plastic wrap from the pie pan. Reheat the quiche in the oven or microwave.

PER SERVING	
Calories	778
Protein	28 g
Fat	58 g
Carbohydrates	35 g
Fibre	1 g
Iron	2 mg
Calcium	580 mg
Sodium	788 mg

Side Dish Idea

Pecan and arugula salad

In a salad bowl, whisk 60 ml (¼ cup) olive oil, 15 ml (1 tbsp) lemon juice and 15 ml (1 tbsp) Dijon mustard. Season with salt and pepper. Add 750 ml (3 cups) arugula and 125 ml (½ cup) pecan halves. Stir. Sprinkle with 125 ml (½ cup) shaved parmesan.

Lean ground beef ①
450 g (1 lb)

Frozen mixed vegetables ②
500 ml (2 cups)

Parsley ③
chopped
60 ml (¼ cup)

Mashed potatoes ④
1 container (680 g)

Cheese spread ⑤
125 ml (½ cup)

Easy Shepherd's Pie

Prep time: **15 minutes** • Cook time: **20 minutes** • Serves: **4**

Preparation

Preheat the oven to 205°C (400°F).

Heat a little olive oil in a pot over medium heat. Cook the ground beef for 3 to 4 minutes, breaking up the meat with a wooden spoon, until it is no longer pink.

Add the diced vegetables and cook for 5 to 6 minutes. Season with salt and pepper. Add the parsley.

Grease a 20 cm (8 in) baking dish and transfer the meat and vegetables into it. Cover with mashed potatoes. Bake for 20 to 25 minutes.

Remove the dish from the oven and let it cool slightly on the counter, then refrigerate to cool completely.

Cover the dish with plastic wrap and then aluminum foil. Place the dish in the freezer.

The night before your meal, let the dish thaw out in the refrigerator.

When ready to eat, remove the aluminum foil and plastic wrap from the baking dish. Reheat the shepherd's pie in the oven or microwave.

Melt the cheese spread in the microwave.

Top each portion with the cheese spread before serving.

PER SERVING	
Calories	500
Protein	30 g
Fat	29 g
Carbohydrates	41 g
Fibre	6 g
Iron	4 mg
Calcium	202 mg
Sodium	1,223 mg

Homemade Version

Mashed potatoes

Peel and dice 6 potatoes. Place in a large saucepan and cover with cold water. Bring to a boil over medium heat and cook for 18 to 20 minutes, until tender. Drain. Mash the potatoes with 125 ml (½ cup) warm milk and 30 ml (2 tbsp) butter. Season with salt and pepper.

4 potatoes
cut into cubes

①

2% milk
125 ml (½ cup)

②

Salmon
fillet
400 g (about 1 lb)
skin removed

③

**Cold water shrimp
or small shrimp**
150 g (250 ml)

④

Pie dough
750 g (1 ⅔ lb)

⑤

ALSO NEEDED:
➤ **Butter**
30 ml (2 tbsp)

➤ **Egg**
1 yolk beaten
with a little water

OPTIONAL:
➤ **3 green onions**
chopped

Mini Salmon and Shrimp Pies

Prep time: **15 minutes** • Cook time: **40 minutes** • Yields: **6 pies, 13 cm (5 in) each**

Preparation

Preheat the oven to 205°C (400°F).

In a pot, place the potatoes and cover with cold, salted water. Bring to a boil and cook for 15 to 20 minutes, until tender. Drain and mash the potatoes with milk, butter, and green onions, if desired. Season with salt and pepper.

Place the salmon on a sheet of aluminum foil. Season with salt and pepper and baste with olive oil. Fold the paper to form a sealed envelope. Bake for 10 to 12 minutes.

Cut the salmon into pieces and add it to the mashed potatoes with the shrimp. Set aside.

Roll the dough out on a floured surface. Cut 6 circles, 15.5 cm (6 ½ in) in diameter each and 6 circles, 13 cm (5 in) in diameter each.

Press the larger rounds into 6 aluminum pie plates, 13 cm (5 in) in diameter. Divide the filling among the pie plates.

Dampen the edges of the bottom pie crust and cover the pies with the smaller rounds. Seal the edges. Cut slits in the surface of the dough in a few places and brush with egg yolk.

Bake for 25 to 30 minutes, until the crust is lightly golden. Remove from the oven and let the pies cool slightly on the counter, then refrigerate to cool completely.

Cover each pie with aluminum foil and place them in freezer bags. Remove the air from the bags and seal them. Place the bags in the freezer.

The night before your meal, let the pies thaw out in the refrigerator.

When ready to eat, remove the aluminum foil from the pies. Reheat in the oven or microwave.

PER SERVING	
Calories	891
Protein	29 g
Fat	46 g
Carbohydrates	85 g
Fibre	5 g
Iron	3 mg
Calcium	88 mg
Sodium	663 mg

Healthy Choice

Cold water shrimp: nutritious and delicious!

Cold water shrimp pack an impressive nutritional punch! One 75 g serving has 60% of our recommended daily intake of essential fatty acids, and is also an excellent source of omega-3 fatty acids. What's more, cold water shrimp are high in protein, vitamin E and coenzyme Q10 (an antioxidant compound). Another plus: unlike frozen shrimp, they do not contain sulfites. So what are you waiting for? Add cold water shrimp to your favourite seafood recipes today!

Tilapia
4 fillets
150 g (⅓ lb)
each
1

2 eggs
2

Plain breadcrumbs
250 ml (1 cup)
3

Tomato pesto or sun-dried tomato pesto
15 ml (1 tbsp)
4

Herbes de Provence
10 ml (2 tsp)
5

ALSO NEEDED:
➤ **Flour**
80 ml (⅓ cup)

➤ **2% milk**
30 ml (2 tbsp)

OPTIONAL:
➤ **1 lemon**
sliced into four wedges

Tilapia Milanese

Prep time: **15 minutes** • Cook time: **4 minutes** • Serves: **4**

Preparation

Cut each fish fillet into thirds, widthwise.

Set out three deep plates. In the first, pour in the flour. In the second, whisk the eggs and milk, then season with salt and pepper. In the third, mix the breadcrumbs with the pesto and herbes de Provence.

Coat the fish strips in flour, shaking them afterward to remove excess flour. Dunk the floured strips into the egg mix, then coat them in breadcrumbs.

Heat a little olive oil in a frying pan over medium heat. Brown the tilapia strips for 2 to 3 minutes on each side. Dry them on paper towels.

Let them cool slightly on the counter, then refrigerate to cool completely.

Place the tilapia sticks in a large freezer bag. Remove the air from the bag and seal it. Place the bag in the freezer.

The night before your meal, let the bag thaw out in the refrigerator.

When ready to eat, reheat the tilapia sticks in the oven or microwave.

Serve with lemon wedges, if desired.

PER SERVING	
Calories	428
Protein	39 g
Fat	16 g
Carbohydrates	31 g
Fibre	2 g
Iron	3 mg
Calcium	99 mg
Sodium	389 mg

Side Dish Idea

Caper tartar sauce

In a bowl, mix 125 ml (½ cup) mayonnaise, 15 ml (1 tbsp) chopped capers and 15 ml (1 tbsp) chopped chives.

California blend frozen vegetables
500 ml (2 cups)
①

Sour cream (14%)
250 ml (1 cup)
②

Chicken
cooked and sliced
500 ml (2 cups)
③

Brown rice
cooked
500 ml (2 cups)
④

Cheddar
shredded
500 ml (2 cups)
⑤

ALSO NEEDED:
➤ **Chicken stock**
250 ml (1 cup)
➤ **Italian seasoning**
15 ml (1 tbsp)

OPTIONAL:
➤ **Basil**
chopped
60 ml (¼ cup)

Creamy Chicken and Brown Rice Gratin

Prep time: **15 minutes** • Cook time: **25 minutes** • Serves: 4

Preparation

In a bowl, mix the vegetables, sour cream, chicken, rice, stock, Italian seasoning and basil, if desired. Season with salt and pepper.

Grease a 20 cm (8 in) square baking dish and transfer the ingredients to it. Smooth out the surface and sprinkle with cheddar.

Cover the dish with plastic wrap and then aluminum foil. Place the dish in the freezer.

The night before your meal, let the gratin thaw out in the refrigerator.

When ready to cook, preheat the oven to 205°C (400°F).

Remove the aluminum foil and plastic wrap from the dish. Bake for 25 to 30 minutes.

Remove from the oven and let rest for 5 to 10 minutes before serving.

PER SERVING	
Calories	617
Protein	47 g
Fat	32 g
Carbohydrates	34 g
Fibre	4 g
Iron	2 mg
Calcium	539 mg
Sodium	812 mg

5•15 Tip

Brown rice, faster!

Brown rice is a nutritional powerhouse, but we often shun it because of how long it takes to cook (about 45 minutes). If you're impatient at the very thought, just put the rice on first and then you can take the time to prepare the rest of the ingredients. Another tip: double the quantity and freeze the rest for future meals. Want an even faster option? Choose parboiled brown rice, it's pre-cooked, which means it's ready in 15 to 20 minutes.

Salmon
fillets
400 g (about 1 lb)
skin removed and cut
into small cubes

1

Frozen chopped spinach
thawed and drained
1 bag (500 g)

2

Ricotta
½ container (475 g)

3

6 fresh lasagna sheets

4

Tomato sauce
625 ml (2 ½ cups)

5

ALSO NEEDED:
➤ **1 egg**
beaten

OPTIONAL:
➤ **Mozzarella**
shredded
375 ml (1 ½ cups)

Salmon Cannelloni

Prep time: **15 minutes** • Cook time: **20 minutes** • Serves: **4**

Preparation

In a bowl, mix the salmon with the spinach, ricotta and egg. Season with salt and pepper.

Cut the lasagna sheets into thirds, lengthwise. Place some of the filling at the base of each noodle and roll.

Pour half of the sauce into a baking dish. Place the cannelloni in the dish, with the closure facing downward. Top with the rest of the sauce and mozzarella, if desired.

Cover the baking dish with plastic wrap and then aluminum foil. Place the dish in the freezer.

The night before your meal, let the cannelloni thaw out in the refrigerator.

When you are ready to cook, preheat the oven to 205°C (400°F).

Remove the aluminum foil and plastic wrap from the baking dish. Put the aluminum foil back on. Bake for 15 to 20 minutes.

Remove the aluminum foil and cook for another 5 minutes.

PER SERVING	
Calories	808
Protein	53 g
Fat	36 g
Carbohydrates	69 g
Fibre	10 g
Iron	6 mg
Calcium	625 mg
Sodium	1,301 mg

Mix It Up

Replace the salmon

Feel like reinventing this salmon-based recipe? Try it with trout! The delicate, tender texture of trout makes for an incredible meal. Shrimp are also a great substitute for this sea-inspired dish!

Pizza dough ①
450 g (1 lb)

Pizza sauce ②
250 ml (1 cup)

Mozzarella ③
shredded
500 ml (2 cups)

4 Italian tomatoes ④
sliced

Basil ⑤
a few leaves

Margherita Pizza

Prep time: **15 minutes** • Cook time: **10 minutes** • Yields: **4 pizzas, 20 cm (8 in) each**

Preparation

Preheat the oven to 205°C (400°F).

Divide the dough into 4 balls. Roll out each ball into a circle, 20 cm (8 in) in diameter, keeping the dough rather thick.

Place the circles on pizza pans or baking dishes. Brush the dough with pizza sauce, and top with mozzarella and tomatoes.

Bake for 10 to 12 minutes, until the dough is golden-brown. Remove the pizzas from the oven. Let them cool slightly on the counter, then refrigerate to cool completely.

Wrap each pizza with plastic wrap and then aluminum foil. Place the pizzas in the freezer.

The night before your meal, let the pizzas thaw out in the refrigerator.

When ready to eat, remove the plastic wrap and aluminum foil, and reheat the pizzas in the oven or microwave.

Sprinkle the pizzas with the basil leaves before serving.

PER SERVING	
Calories	560
Protein	24 g
Fat	24 g
Carbohydrates	60 g
Fibre	4 g
Iron	5 mg
Calcium	385 mg
Sodium	776 mg

5•15 Tip

Use different kinds of breads for the pizza base

Don't have any pizza dough? Why not substitute it with naan, tortillas, English muffins or pita breads? These options add some variety to your menu and might even offer a solution to all those leftovers... a delicious pizza!

Mild Italian sausages
450 g (1 lb)

20 mini bell peppers
various colours

Marinara sauce
625 ml (2 ½ cups)

Italian seasoning
15 ml (1 tbsp)

Mozzarella or smoked mozzarella
shredded
375 ml (1 ½ cups)

Sausage-stuffed Mini Peppers

Prep time: **15 minutes** • Cook time: **25 minutes** • Serves: **6**

Preparation

Remove the casing from the sausages.

Cut the mini bell peppers in half.

Stuff the peppers with the sausage meat.

In a bowl, mix the marinara sauce with the Italian seasoning. Season with salt and pepper.

Grease a 20 cm (8 in) square baking dish, then spread a little marinara sauce in the bottom. Lay the stuffed peppers in the dish, and top with the rest of the sauce. Sprinkle with mozzarella.

Cover the dish with plastic wrap and then aluminum foil. Place the dish in the freezer.

The night before your meal, let the dish thaw out in the refrigerator.

When ready to cook, preheat the oven to 205°C (400°F).

Remove the aluminum foil and plastic wrap from the dish. Bake for 25 to 30 minutes.

PER SERVING	
Calories	416
Protein	20 g
Fat	25 g
Carbohydrates	28 g
Fibre	7 g
Iron	2 mg
Calcium	224 mg
Sodium	1,243 mg

Mix It Up

Cook with mini bell peppers

There's nothing like mini bell peppers to brighten up a plate! They inject a beautiful dose of colour into any dish while adding flavour just as sweet as that of their larger counterparts. These bright little peppers are also an excellent source of vitamin C. Look for them in the supermarket, where they come in packages of 7 to 10 and a variety of colours.

Alfredo sauce ①
light
625 ml (2 ½ cups)

Parmesan ②
shredded
375 ml (1 ½ cups)

Shallots ③
chopped
60 ml (¼ cup)

Chicken ④
4 skinless breasts
cut into small cubes

Broccoli ⑤
1 stalk
cut into small florets

ALSO NEEDED:
➤ **Fresh herbs
of your choice**
(parsley, basil, etc.)
chopped
125 ml (½ cup)

➤ **Garlic**
minced
15 ml (1 tbsp)

OPTIONAL:
➤ **Panko breadcrumbs**
125 ml (½ cup)

Chicken Alfredo

Prep time: **15 minutes** • Cook time: **35 minutes** • Serves: **6**

Preparation

In a bowl, mix the Alfredo sauce, shallots, herbs, garlic and half of the parmesan. Season with pepper.

Add the chicken and broccoli. Stir.

Transfer the preparation to a 33 cm x 23 cm (13 in x 9 in) baking dish.

Sprinkle with the rest of the parmesan and the panko breadcrumbs, if desired.

Cover the dish with plastic wrap and then aluminum foil. Place the dish in the freezer.

The night before your meal, let the dish thaw out in the refrigerator.

When ready to cook, preheat the oven to 205°C (400°F).

Remove the aluminum foil and plastic wrap. Bake for 35 to 40 minutes, until the chicken is cooked through.

PER SERVING	
Calories	356
Protein	39 g
Fat	15 g
Carbohydrates	14 g
Fibre	1 g
Iron	1 mg
Calcium	427 mg
Sodium	1,062 mg

Healthy Choice

A tasty and healthy casserole!

This one-dish meal brings together three of the four food groups: a vegetable (broccoli), a dairy product (cheese) and a source of protein (chicken). It's full of nutrients too, with vitamins C and K as well as lutein and zeaxanthin (two carotenoids with antioxidant properties), thanks to the broccoli. Get your fill of vitamins and minerals with this easy and delicious dish!

Frozen diced vegetable mix
thawed and drained
250 ml (1 cup)

1

Lean ground beef
450 g (1 lb)

2

Frozen chopped spinach
thawed and drained
1 bag (500 g)

3

Light ricotta cheese (5%)
250 ml (1 cup)

4

Monterey Jack
shredded
250 ml (1 cup)

5

ALSO NEEDED:
➤ **Garlic**
minced
15 ml (1 tbsp)

OPTIONAL:
➤ **Paprika**
15 ml (1 tbsp)

Beef, Spinach and Ricotta Gratin

Prep time: **15 minutes** • Cook time: **20 minutes** • Serves: 4

Preparation

Heat a little olive oil in a pot over medium heat. Cook the diced vegetables and garlic for 2 to 3 minutes.

Add the ground beef. Season with salt and pepper, and stir well. Cook for 4 to 5 minutes, breaking up the meat with a wooden spoon, until it is no longer pink. Add the paprika, if desired.

Transfer the meat and vegetables to four ramekins or one baking dish. Top with spinach and ricotta. Cover with Monterey Jack.

Cover the ramekins or dish with plastic wrap and then aluminum foil. Place in the freezer.

The night before your meal, let the gratin thaw out in the refrigerator.

When ready to cook, preheat the oven to 205°C (400°F).

Remove the aluminum foil and plastic wrap from the ramekins. Bake for 25 to 30 minutes.

PER SERVING	
Calories	558
Protein	43 g
Fat	38 g
Carbohydrates	14 g
Fibre	6 g
Iron	6 mg
Calcium	621 mg
Sodium	458 mg

Healthy Choice

Ricotta

With its rich and creamy texture, ricotta is a star ingredient in our gratins. It's the perfect substitute for cream cheese, sour cream and mascarpone in cheesy dishes—and it's healthy too! And thanks to its subtle flavour, ricotta pairs perfectly with any ingredient so don't hesitate to add it to your favorite dishes!

Sole
12 fillets

1

Basil
12 leaves

2

Marinara sauce
400 ml (about 1 ⅔ cups)

3

Sun-dried tomato vinaigrette
60 ml (¼ cup)

4

Italien blend shredded cheese
375 ml (1 ½ cups)

5

Italian Sole Fillets

Prep time: **10 minutes** • Cook time: **25 minutes** • Serves: 4

Preparation

Place the sole fillets in a baking dish. Arrange the basil leaves on the fillets and roll them up.

In a bowl, mix the marinara sauce with the vinaigrette and the olives, if desired. Pour the sauce over the fillets. Cover with cheese.

Cover the dish with plastic wrap and then aluminum foil. Place the dish in the freezer.

The night before your meal, let the dish thaw out in the refrigerator.

When ready to cook, preheat the oven to 205°C (400°F).

Remove the aluminum foil and plastic wrap from the dish. Bake for 25 to 30 minutes.

PER SERVING	
Calories	486
Protein	43 g
Fat	30 g
Carbohydrates	11 g
Fibre	2 g
Iron	2 mg
Calcium	435 mg
Sodium	1,200 mg

Homemade Version

Marinara sauce

Heat 30 ml (2 tbsp) olive oil in a pot over medium heat. Sear 1 chopped onion and 15 ml (1 tbsp) minced garlic for 1 to 2 minutes. Add 1 can (796 ml) Italian tomatoes with the juice, 30 ml (2 tbsp) tomato paste and 15 ml (1 tbsp) sugar. Season with salt and pepper. Bring to a boil, then cover and simmer for 25 minutes over low heat. Add 60 ml (¼ cup) minced basil. Stir and simmer for 5 minutes. For a smooth and consistent sauce, puree with an immersion blender or electric mixer.

OPTIONAL:
➤ **16 green olives**

Pizza dough ①
500 g (about 1 lb)

BBQ sauce ②
375 ml (1 ½ cups)

Chicken ③
cooked and chopped
500 ml (2 cups)

1 yellow bell pepper ④
diced

Pizza mozzarella ⑤
shredded
500 ml (2 cups)

ALSO NEEDED:
➤ **1 onion**
diced

OPTIONAL:
➤ **Blue cheese**
crumbled
125 g (about ¼ lb)

BBQ Chicken Pizza

Prep time: **15 minutes** • Cook time: **20 minutes** • Serves: **6**

Preparation

Preheat the oven to 205°C (400°F).

Stretch out the dough on a lightly floured surface into a rectangle, 33 cm x 23 cm (13 in x 9 in).

Place the dough on a baking sheet. Brush with half of the BBQ sauce.

Top with the chicken, bell pepper, onion and mozzarella. Drizzle the rest of the BBQ sauce over the pizza, and sprinkle with blue cheese, if desired.

Bake for 20 to 25 minutes. Remove the tray from the oven and let the pizza cool slightly on the counter, then refrigerate to cool completely.

Wrap the pizza in plastic wrap and then aluminum foil. Place the pizza in the freezer.

The night before your meal, let the pizza thaw out in the refrigerator.

When ready to eat, remove the aluminum foil and plastic wrap and reheat the pizza in the oven or microwave.

PER SERVING	
Calories	630
Protein	36 g
Fat	18 g
Carbohydrates	43 g
Fibre	2 g
Iron	3 mg
Calcium	347 mg
Sodium	1,326 mg

Healthy Choice

The essentials for a healthy pizza

Who said pizza night has to stay stuck in its pepperoni-and-cheese rut? The possibilities are endless, setting the stage for a fun exercise in culinary creativity. For a pizza that's both tasty and healthy, think lean proteins like chicken, shrimp or lean ground beef. Then top it off with lots of colourful vegetables to give your body all the dietary fibre it needs.

1 butternut squash ①

Smoked maple ham ②
sliced
250 g (about ½ lb)

Cheddar ③
shredded
375 ml (1 ½ cups)

Cooking cream (15%) ④
250 ml (1 cup)

Parsley ⑤
chopped
60 ml (¼ cup)

ALSO NEEDED:
➤ **1 egg**
➤ **Flour**
30 ml (2 tbsp)

OPTIONAL:
➤ **Nutmeg**
2.5 ml (½ tsp)

Squash and Ham Gratin

Prep time: **15 minutes** • Cook time: **36 minutes** • Serves: **6**

Preparation

Peel the squash and remove the seeds. Slice the squash into thin slices.

Grease a 20 cm (8 in) square baking dish. Place half of the squash slices into the dish.

Cover the squash with the ham slices and half of the cheese.

In a bowl, whisk the egg, flour, cream, parsley and nutmeg, if desired.

Pour half of the mix into the baking dish. Cover with the rest of the squash, and pour in the rest of the cream preparation. Sprinkle with the remaining cheese.

Cover the dish with plastic wrap and then aluminum foil. Place the dish in the freezer.

The night before your meal, let the gratin thaw out in the refrigerator.

When ready to cook, preheat the oven to 190°C (375°F).

Remove the aluminum foil and plastic wrap from the dish. Put the aluminum foil back on the dish. Bake for 18 to 20 minutes.

Remove the aluminum foil and cook for another 18 to 20 minutes.

PER SERVING	
Calories	303
Protein	31 g
Fat	20 g
Carbohydrates	18 g
Fibre	3 g
Iron	2 mg
Calcium	329 mg
Sodium	525 mg

Chef's Secret

The best cheeses for gratins

The best cheeses for making gratins are firm or semi-firm kinds. The classics are mozzarella, cheddar, Gruyère, Emmenthal and raclette cheese. And you can always swap them up to add something new to your recipes! For the final touch, don't forget to let your gratin rest for a few minutes before serving to give the cheese time to stop bubbling and settle.

5 to 6 yellow potatoes ①

Garlic and herbs cheese spread ②
2 containers
(150 g each)

Cooking cream (15%) ③
500 ml (2 cups)

White wine ④
125 ml (½ cup)

Smoked salmon ⑤
2 packages
(140 g each)
cut into pieces

Salmon Potato Gratin

Prep time: **15 minutes** • Cook time: **20 minutes** • Serves: **4**

Preparation

Peel the potatoes, then use a mandoline to cut them into thin slices.

Place the potato slices in a pot. Cover with cold, salted water. Bring to a boil and cook for 2 minutes. Drain.

In the same pot, place the cheese, cream and white wine. Bring to a boil, stirring.

Remove the pot from the heat and add the potatoes and smoked salmon. Season with salt and pepper, and stir well.

Grease a 20 cm (8 in) square baking dish, and transfer the prepared salmon and potatoes into it. Even out the surface.

Let the preparation cool slightly on the counter, then refrigerate to cool completely.

Cover the dish with plastic wrap and then aluminum foil. Place the dish in the freezer.

The night before your meal, let the dish thaw out in the refrigerator.

When ready to cook, preheat the oven to 205°C (400°F).

Remove the aluminum foil and plastic wrap from the dish. Bake for 20 to 25 minutes.

PER SERVING	
Calories	940
Protein	36 g
Fat	58 g
Carbohydrates	66 g
Fibre	4 g
Iron	3 mg
Calcium	225 mg
Sodium	803 mg

Chef's Secret

Choose the right baking dish

To make a perfect gratin, you need a good baking dish. Choose a baking dish made out of ceramic, glass (like Pyrex) or enamelled cast iron so that it resists the heat of the oven. The rectangular models (13 in x 9 in) are great for gratins. You should also use one with high sides (3 to 4 in) to properly contain creamy sauces!

Panko breadcrumbs ①
250 ml (1 cup)

Light parmesan ②
grated
60 ml (¼ cup)

Italian seasoning ③
30 ml (2 tbsp)

Lemon zest ④
15 ml (1 tbsp)

Chicken ⑤
4 skinless breasts

OPTIONAL:
➤ **Mozzarella**
shredded
250 ml (1 cup)
➤ **Basil**
4 leaves

ALSO NEEDED:
➤ **Flour**
60 ml (¼ cup)
➤ **2 eggs**

Lemon Parmesan Chicken

Prep time: **15 minutes** • Cook time: **12 minutes** • Serves: **4**

Preparation

Preheat the oven to 205°C (400°F).

In a bowl, mix the breadcrumbs, parmesan, Italian seasoning and zest.

Set out three deep plates. Put the flour in the first. Beat the eggs in the second. Pour the breadcrumb mix in the third.

Cover the chicken breasts in flour, dip them into the beaten eggs and cover them with breadcrumbs.

Heat a little canola oil in a large pan over medium heat. Brown the chicken breasts for 2 to 3 minutes on each side.

Place the breasts on a baking sheet lined with parchment paper. Garnish each breast with mozzarella, if desired.

Bake for 8 to 10 minutes, until the chicken is no longer pink in the centre.

Remove the baking dish from the oven. Let it cool slightly on the counter, then refrigerate to cool completely.

Place the chicken breasts in an airtight container. Place the container in the freezer.

The night before your meal, let the chicken breasts thaw out in the refrigerator.

When ready to eat, reheat the chicken breasts in the oven or microwave. Garnish with basil, if desired.

PER SERVING	
Calories	447
Protein	54 g
Fat	15 g
Carbohydrates	20 g
Fibre	1 g
Iron	2 mg
Calcium	350 mg
Sodium	557 mg

Side Dish Idea

Green bean and cherry tomato salad

In a bowl, mix 45 ml (3 tbsp) white balsamic vinegar with 45 ml (3 tbsp) olive oil and 10 ml (2 tsp) honey. Add 300 g (⅔ lb) cooked green beans and 500 ml (2 cups) cherry tomatoes of various colours, cut in half. Season with salt and pepper, and stir.

Zucchinis
2 green and 2 yellow
①

Mushrooms
chopped
1 container (227 g)
②

Shredded four cheese blend
500 ml (2 cups)
③

Cooking cream (15%)
250 ml (1 cup)
④

18 cherry tomatoes
cut in half
⑤

ALSO NEEDED:
➤ **1 onion**
chopped
➤ **2 eggs**

OPTIONAL:
➤ **Parsley**
chopped
60 ml (¼ cup)

Zucchini Gratin

Prep time: **15 minutes** • Cook time: **25 minutes** • Serves: **4**

Preparation

Cut the zucchinis into thin rounds.

Melt a little butter in a pot over medium heat. Cook the mushrooms and onion for 2 to 3 minutes. Remove from the heat and let cool.

In a large bowl, beat the eggs, cream, mushrooms, onion, half the shredded cheese, and parsley, if desired. Add three quarters of the zucchini rounds. Season with salt and pepper. Stir well.

Grease a baking dish and transfer the preparation into it.

Arrange the remaining zucchini rounds on top of the dish. Top with cherry tomatoes, then cover with the rest of the cheese.

Cover the dish with plastic wrap and then aluminum foil. Place the dish in the freezer.

The night before your meal, let the dish thaw out in the refrigerator.

When ready to cook, preheat the oven to 205°C (400°F).

Remove the aluminum foil and plastic wrap from the dish. Bake for 25 to 30 minutes.

PER SERVING	
Calories	431
Protein	22 g
Fat	33 g
Carbohydrates	18 g
Fibre	4 g
Iron	2 mg
Calcium	468 mg
Sodium	348 mg

5•15 Tip

How to pick the best zucchini

Zucchini, also known as courgette, can be found year-round in the vegetable aisle at the supermarket. Choose firm and intact zucchini with smooth skin and a vibrant colour. Too small and it'll lack flavour; too big, and it'll be fibrous and bitter. And most importantly, watch out for bruises or blemishes!

2 small zucchinis 1

Marinara sauce 2
625 ml (2 ½ cups)

Basil 3
chopped
60 ml (¼ cup)

Mozzarella 4
shredded
500 ml (2 cups)

Beef ravioli 5
frozen
350 g (about ¾ lb)

ALSO NEEDED:
➤ **Oregano leaves**
30 ml (2 tbsp)

Ravioli and Zucchini Lasagna

Prep time: **15 minutes** • Cook time: **40 minutes** • Serves: **4**

Preparation

Use a mandoline or vegetable peeler to cut the zucchinis into thin slices, lengthwise.

Pour a little of the marinara sauce in a 20 cm (8 in) square baking dish. Line the bottom of the dish with the zucchinis.

Layer with a third of the remaining marinara sauce. Garnish with a little basil and oregano. Cover with a fourth of the mozzarella. Place a third of the ravioli side by side into the dish. Repeat this step two more times, and then cover with the remaining mozzarella.

Cover the dish in plastic wrap and aluminum foil. Place it in the freezer.

The night before your meal, let the dish thaw out in the refrigerator.

When ready to cook, preheat the oven to 205°C (400°F).

Remove the aluminum foil and plastic wrap from the dish. Bake for 40 to 45 minutes.

PER SERVING	
Calories	542
Protein	27 g
Fat	29 g
Carbohydrates	48 g
Fibre	8 g
Iron	2 mg
Calcium	506 mg
Sodium	955 mg

Mix It Up

Use other kinds of ravioli!

Looking to change up the flavours of this recipe? Grocery stores offer several types of stuffed ravioli: spinach and ricotta, mushroom, cheese, herb, etc. Choose whatever sounds tastiest!

Cooking cream (15%) ①
500 ml (2 cups)

Brie cheese ②
rind removed
150 g (⅓ lb)

Salmon ③
fillets
750 g (1 ⅔ lb)
skin removed and cut
into small cubes

6 fresh lasagna sheets ④

Mozzarella ⑤
shredded
375 ml (1 ½ cups)

OPTIONAL:
➤ **Lemon zest**
15 ml (1 tbsp)
➤ **Dill**
chopped
45 ml (3 tbsp)

Salmon Lasagna

Prep time: **15 minutes** • Cook time: **35 minutes** • Serves: **6**

Preparation

Preheat the oven to 190°C (375°F).

In a pot, heat the cream and Brie over medium heat, stirring until it starts to simmer. Add the salmon. Remove from heat.

Add the zest and dill, if desired. Season with salt and pepper.

Pour a little of the salmon sauce in a 20 cm (8 in) square baking dish and cover with two sheets of lasagna. Add half of the salmon sauce and cover with two more lasagna sheets. Repeat, and then cover with mozzarella.

Cook in the oven for 35 to 40 minutes, until the noodles are tender.

Remove the baking dish from the oven. Let it cool slightly on the counter, then refrigerate to cool completely.

Cover the dish with plastic wrap and aluminum foil. Place it in the freezer.

The night before your meal, let the lasagna thaw out in the refrigerator.

When ready to eat, remove the aluminum foil and the plastic wrap from the dish. Reheat the lasagna in the oven or microwave.

PER SERVING	
Calories	749
Protein	43 g
Fat	46 g
Carbohydrates	38 g
Fibre	2 g
Iron	1 mg
Calcium	316 mg
Sodium	386 mg

Side Dish Idea

Fresh salad

In a salad bowl, whisk 60 ml (¼ cup) olive oil with 15 ml (1 tbsp) lemon juice and 15 ml (1 tbsp) chopped parsley. Season with salt and pepper. Add 16 yellow cherry tomatoes, cut in half, ½ red onion, chopped, and 500 ml (2 cups) mesclun. Stir.

Whole wheat orecchiette ①
or any other
short pasta
500 ml (2 cups)

3 leeks ②
white part
chopped

Chorizo ③
diced
80 g (about 2 ¾ oz)

Ricotta ④
220 g (about ½ lb)

Pecans ⑤
chopped
45 ml (3 tbsp)

ALSO NEEDED:
➤ **1 onion**
chopped
➤ **1 egg**

OPTIONAL:
➤ **Garlic**
2 cloves
minced

Chorizo and Ricotta Pasta Bake

Prep time: **15 minutes** • Cook time: **30 minutes** • Serves: **6**

PER SERVING	
Calories	355
Protein	16 g
Fat	17 g
Carbohydrates	39 g
Fibre	6 g
Iron	3 mg
Calcium	132 mg
Sodium	295 mg

Preparation

Cook the pasta *al dente* in a large pot of boiling, salted water. Drain, keeping about 250 ml (1 cup) cooking water.

Heat a little olive oil in a non-stick frying pan over medium heat. Cook the leeks, chorizo, onion, and garlic, if desired, for 5 minutes.

Add 80 ml (⅓ cup) of cooking water and cook for another 5 minutes, until the leeks are tender.

Season with salt and pepper. Add the pasta and stir.

Pour the preparation in a baking dish, 30 cm x 20 cm (12 in x 8 in). Let the pasta cool slightly on the counter, and then refrigerate to cool completely.

In a small bowl, mix the ricotta and egg. Pour over the pasta, then sprinkle with pecans.

Cover the baking dish with plastic wrap and aluminum foil. Place the dish in the freezer.

The night before your meal, let the dish thaw out in the refrigerator.

When ready to cook, preheat the oven to 180°C (350°F).

Remove the aluminum foil and plastic wrap from the baking dish. Bake for 30 minutes, until the cheese is golden-brown.

Learn More

Orecchiette

Never heard of orecchiette? These little noodles are similar to pasta shells. Because they look like little ears and are originally from Italy (in Italy, orecchio means "ear"), these noodles were named orecchiette, or "little ears". Ideal in gratins or simply served with a creamy sauce, orecchiette bring a touch of light-hearted Italian flavour to the menu!

Shrimp, Scallop and Cauliflower Gratin

Prep time: **15 minutes** • Cook time: **5 minutes** • Serves: **4**

1 cauliflower
cut into small florets

Butter
60 ml (¼ cup)

2% milk
625 ml (2 ½ cups)

Mixed frozen shrimp and scallops
thawed
2 bags (340 g each)

Mozzarella
shredded
250 ml (1 cup)

ALSO NEEDED:
➤ **1 onion**
chopped
➤ **Flour**
80 ml (⅓ cup)

OPTIONAL:
➤ **Chives**
chopped
45 ml (3 tbsp)

Preparation

In a pot of boiling, salted water, cook the cauliflower for 4 minutes. Rinse under cold water and drain.

In the same pot, melt the butter over medium heat. Sear the onion for 1 minute.

Add the flour and cook for 1 minute, stirring, without letting it brown.

Pour in the milk and stir. Heat until it starts to simmer, whisking.

Add the seafood, cauliflower, and chives, if desired. Season with salt and pepper. Cook over medium heat for 2 to 3 minutes.

Pour the preparation into a baking dish or four ramekins. Let it cool slightly on the counter, then refrigerate to cool completely.

Sprinkle with mozzarella.

Cover the dish with plastic wrap and then aluminum foil. Place the dish in the freezer.

The night before your meal, let the gratin thaw out in the refrigerator.

When ready to cook, preheat the oven to 205°C (400°F).

Remove the aluminum foil and plastic wrap from the dish. Bake for 15 to 20 minutes, or until the cheese is golden-brown.

PER SERVING	
Calories	455
Protein	37 g
Fat	24 g
Carbohydrates	29 g
Fibre	4 g
Iron	1 mg
Calcium	449 mg
Sodium	1,193 mg

Side Dish Idea

Lemon parsley farfalle

Cook 1 litre (4 cups) farfalle pasta (bowties) *al dente* in a pot of boiling, salted water. Drain. Heat 45 ml (3 tbsp) olive oil in a pot over medium heat. Cook 5 ml (1 tsp) minced garlic with 30 ml (2 tbsp) chopped parsley and 15 ml (1 tbsp) lemon zest for 2 minutes. Mix in the pasta. Season with salt and pepper.

Cheddar
shredded
500 ml (2 cups)
①

Frozen chopped spinach
thawed and drained
1 bag (500 g)
②

Chicken
cooked and shredded
750 ml (3 cups)
③

6 fresh lasagna sheets ④

Tomato sauce
500 ml (2 cups)
⑤

OPTIONAL:
➤ **Garlic**
2 cloves
coarsely chopped

➤ **Parmesan**
grated
60 ml (¼ cup)

ALSO NEEDED:
➤ **1 egg**

Chicken Cannelloni

Prep time: **15 minutes** • Cook time: **20 minutes** • Serves: **6**

Preparation

In a food processor, place half of the cheddar with the spinach and egg. Add the garlic and parmesan, if desired. Mix until smooth.

Transfer the preparation into a large bowl and add the chicken. Stir.

Preheat the oven to 180°C (350°F).

Cut the lasagna sheets in half to make 12 rectangles.

Place 80 ml (⅓ cup) of the filling at the base of each rectangle and roll.

In a pot, heat the tomato sauce until it starts to simmer.

Cover the bottom of a rectangular baking dish, 33 cm x 23 cm (13 in x 9 in), with a third of the sauce. Place the cannelloni side by side in the baking dish, with the closure facing downward. Layer with the remaining sauce and sprinkle with the remaining cheddar.

Bake for 20 to 25 minutes.

Remove the baking dish from the oven. Let it cool slightly on the counter, then refrigerator to cool completely.

Cover the dish with plastic wrap and aluminum foil. Place it in the freezer.

The night before your meal, let the cannelloni thaw out in the refrigerator.

When ready to eat, remove the aluminum foil and plastic wrap from the dish. Reheat the cannelloni in the oven or microwave.

PER SERVING	
Calories	524
Protein	45 g
Fat	19 g
Carbohydrates	44 g
Fibre	6 g
Iron	4 mg
Calcium	501 mg
Sodium	931 mg

Learn more

Spinach: A super food!

Spinach, a cousin of chard, is particularly rich in vitamins A and B9 (folic acid), as well as several minerals (iron, magnesium). Although it doesn't contain as much iron as was previously thought, this slightly spicy leafy green contains a significant quantity of antioxidant compounds, including lutein and zeaxanthin. In addition to being beneficial to eye health, these carotenoids are thought to help prevent certain types of cancers. Cooked spinach provides about six times more lutein and zeaxanthin than the same portion of raw spinach.

Medium ground beef
450 g (1 lb)

1

Taco seasoning
1 pouch (39 g)

2

3 tomatoes
diced

3

Frozen diced vegetable mix
500 ml (2 cups)

4

Tex-Mex shredded cheese
500 ml (2 cups)

5

ALSO NEEDED:
➤ **Rice**
cooked
1 litre (4 cups)

➤ **Cilantro**
chopped
45 ml (3 tbsp)

OPTIONAL:
➤ **Frozen corn kernels**
250 ml (1 cup)

➤ **Black beans**
rinsed and drained
1 can (540 ml)

Taco Casserole

Prep time: **15 minutes** • Cook time: **30 minutes** • Serves: **6**

Preparation

Heat a little olive oil in a pot over medium heat. Cook the ground beef for 4 to 5 minutes, breaking up the meat with a wooden spoon.

Add the taco seasoning and tomatoes. Bring to a boil.

Transfer the beef preparation to a large bowl. Add the mixed vegetables, rice and cilantro. Add the corn and beans, if desired. Season with salt and pepper. Stir well. Let it cool slightly on the counter, then refrigerate to cool completely.

Grease a 20 cm (8 in) baking dish and transfer the preparation to the dish. Smooth out the surface. Sprinkle with cheese.

Cover the dish with plastic wrap and then aluminum foil. Place the dish in the freezer.

The night before your meal, let the gratin thaw out in the refrigerator.

When ready to cook, preheat the oven to 205°C (400°F).

Remove the aluminum foil and plastic wrap from the dish. Bake for 30 to 35 minutes.

PER SERVING	
Calories	560
Protein	31 g
Fat	23 g
Carbohydrates	55 g
Fibre	6 g
Iron	3 mg
Calcium	64 mg
Sodium	722 mg

Healthy Choice

Legumes: the perfect addition to your recipes!

There's a lot to be said for legumes! There are many different kinds, including the delicious black bean, and they are not only affordable but also a source of plant-based protein, fibre, vitamins and minerals (iron, zinc and B-complex vitamins)—all of which adds up to make them an unparalleled superfood. With their protein and fibre combo, legumes help you feel full and keep your energy levels up until your next meal. Plus, they're low in fat and can be preserved for months without losing their nutritional value.

Pizza dough ①
450 g (1 lb)

Pizza sauce ②
160 ml (⅔ cup)

Pepperoni ③
or salami
sliced
100 g (3 ½ oz)

1 green bell pepper ④
diced

Cheddar ⑤
shredded
500 ml (2 cups)

OPTIONAL:
➤ **Chorizo**
sliced
50 g (1 ¾ oz)
➤ **Black olives**
80 ml (⅓ cup)

ALSO NEEDED:
➤ **1 onion**
diced

Deluxe Homemade Pizza

Prep time: **15 minutes** • Cook time: **20 minutes** • Serves: **6 (2 pizzas, 25 cm - 10 in each)**

Preparation

Preheat the oven to 205°C (400°F).

Divide the dough into two balls. Stretch out each of the balls on a lightly floured surface and form two circles, 25 cm (10 in) in diameter.

Place the dough on one or two pizza pans or baking sheets. Top the dough with sauce, pepperoni, peppers, onion, and chorizo and olives, if desired. Cover with cheese.

Bake for 20 to 25 minutes. Remove the pizzas from the oven and let them cool slightly on the counter, then refrigerate to cool completely.

Wrap each pizzas in plastic wrap and then in aluminum foil. Place the pizzas in the freezer.

The night before your meal, let the pizzas thaw out in the refrigerator.

When ready to eat, remove the aluminum foil and plastic wrap. Reheat the pizzas in the oven or microwave.

PER SERVING	
Calories	491
Protein	23 g
Fat	25 g
Carbohydrates	42 g
Fibre	3 g
Iron	4 mg
Calcium	315 mg
Sodium	1,228 mg

Side Dish Idea

Seasoned oven fries

Wash 5 potatoes and cut them into sticks. Rinse under cold water, drain and pat dry. In a bowl, mix the potatoes with 30 ml (2 tbsp) olive oil, 15 ml (1 tbsp) chopped thyme and 5 ml (1 tsp) paprika. Season with salt. Spread the potatoes out in a single layer on a baking sheet lined with parchment paper. Bake for 20 to 25 minutes at 205°C (400°F).

Lean ground chicken ➊
450 g (1 lb)

Italian blend frozen vegetables ➋
500 ml (2 cups)

Condensed tomato soup ➌
low sodium
1 can (284 ml)

Brown rice ➍
cooked
375 ml (1 ½ cups)

Mozzarella ➎
reduced fat (15 %)
shredded
250 ml (1 cup)

ALSO NEEDED:
➤ **Chicken stock concentrate**
low sodium
15 ml (1 tbsp)

OPTIONAL:
➤ **Curry powder**
15 ml (1 tbsp)

Chicken and Vegetable Gratin

Prep time: **15 minutes** • Cook time: **27 minutes** • Serves: **4**

Preparation

Heat a little olive oil in a pot over medium heat. Cook the chicken with the chicken stock concentrate, stirring. Season with pepper.

Add the vegetables and simmer for 10 minutes, until the chicken is no longer pink. Add the tomato soup, rice, and curry powder if desired. Stir. Simmer for 2 to 3 minutes.

Transfer the preparation into a baking dish. Let it cool slightly on the counter, then refrigerate to cool completely.

Sprinkle the cheese over the preparation. Cover the baking dish with plastic wrap and then aluminum foil. Place the dish in the freezer.

The night before your meal, let the dish thaw out in the refrigerator.

When ready to cook, preheat the oven to 205°C (400°F).

Remove the aluminum foil and plastic wrap from the baking dish. Cook in the oven for 15 minutes, until the cheese has lightly browned.

PER SERVING	
Calories	432
Protein	33 g
Fat	24 g
Carbohydrates	35 g
Fibre	4 g
Iron	3 mg
Calcium	286 mg
Sodium	880 mg

5•15 Tip

Choose your ground meat wisely

Ground beef, pork and chicken are affordable and convenient ingredients that can be used to make a whole host of recipes. If you have to sauté ground meat in a frying pan (for a sauce or tacos, for example), opt for regular ground meat (30% fat), making sure to fully drain it once cooked to remove excess fat. For burgers or meatballs, look for medium (23% fat) or lean (17% fat) ground meats. Leave the extra-lean (10% fat) ground meats for baked dishes, like gratins or meat loaves. Also consider varying the types of ground meat that you use to change things up a little!

Recipes Index

Made by

Publisher of